P9-CZV-469

BRINGING CHRIST TO THE CLASSROOM

Scripture Studies for Educators

CHARISSA DUNN

DESIGN AND PHOTOGRAPHY BY
LORI L. STORIE

BRINGING CHRIST TO THE CLASSROOM
SCRIPTURE STUDIES FOR EDUCATORS

iUniverse books may be ordered through booksellers or by contacting:

iUniverse
1663 Liberty Drive
Bloomington, IN 47403
www.iuniverse.com
1-800-Authors (1-800-288-4677)

ISBN: 978-1-5320-5478-5 (sc)
ISBN: 978-1-5320-5477-8 (e)

Library of Congress Control Number: 2018909646

Print information available on the last page.

iUniverse rev. date: 09/12/2018

DEDICATION

This Bible study is dedicated to several groups of people:

1. Educators in the Dunn and Glenn families whose godly examples encouraged me to pursue the field of education.

2. Faithful instructors who inspired me to give God my best.

3. Student teachers who, over a 20-year period, kept me on my toes, motivated me, and challenged me to seek Christ daily.

My deep gratitude and love go to my parents, John and Wilma Dunn, who, by word and deed, fostered within me and my five siblings, the attitude that we really "... can do all this through him who gives me [us] strength" (**Philippians 4:13**).

CONTENTS

FOREWORD

Bringing Christ to the Classroom is an important book for anyone who is an educator. No matter who you teach or your setting, Charissa's unique insights will be valuable. They'll encourage you and inspire you.

Learning more about Jesus is always good. For educators to see Him as our Teacher enriches our relationship with Him and empowers us in our ministries. Reading familiar Bible passages and applying them to our ministry with Charissa's excellent direction will increase their relevance. The Scripture will be personal and practical. Because she motivates you toward relevant takeaways, you and your students will benefit from your reading of this book. Charissa understands you. She's a teacher, too. I believe you'll come back to these pages often to consider her golden nuggets. I know I will.

Kathy Koch, Ph.D., founder and president of Celebrate Kids, Inc., and the author of six books including *8 Great Smarts: Discover and Nurture Your Child's Intelligences* and *Screens and Teens: Connecting with Our Kids in a Wireless World*

PREFACE

The journey of this Bible study began at a conference where I was introduced to the idea of teaching Christianly. Discussions with Christian educators from other universities inspired me to learn more and integrate conversations about teaching Christianly into weekly meetings with student teachers. These concepts were also embedded into university classes taught at Oklahoma Wesleyan University, on ministry trips to Puerto Rico, and during teacher training in Haiti.

My prayer is that you will use this Bible study as a springboard to provide an additional way of studying Scripture—as a way to extract lessons, encouragement, and inspiration for yourself as both an educator and a follower of Christ.

ACKNOWLEDGEMENTS

I extend my gratitude to those who assisted with this study, specifically Peggy Cauthen and Kourtney Rhoads for their reassurance that this was a worthwhile project, Stephanie Leupp for her assistance in finding resources, Don and Naomi Mueller for hymn title suggestions, Mary Maness for her guidance, advice, and proofreading of an early draft, Gail Richardson for her encouragement and proofreading expertise in the final draft, and Megan England for her assistance with interior images. Special thanks to Jim Dunn for reviewing the manuscript and his gracious and humbling comments.

INTRODUCTION

For twenty years, it was my privilege to supervise and meet weekly with each current group of student teachers enrolled in our teacher training program at Oklahoma Wesleyan University. Throughout those years, God prompted me in developing various aspects of several topics, including "teaching Christianly" and "Jesus, The Master Teacher" for studies and discussions with the student teachers. Because many student teachers indicated these ideas presented them with new perspectives on the connections between Scripture and teaching, I sought direction in making the information available to a wider audience. I hope and pray this Bible study will provide you with new ideas applicable to your position as a Christian educator.

Studying "The Master Teacher"

Someone once said that after reading great literature, we are changed in some way. God's Word is the most significant literature because it changes everything about us as we enter into a personal relationship with our creator. Due to our familiarity with Scripture, it is easy to gloss over the gems that would expand our understanding of God and his creation. Therefore, we need to employ what some call "spiritual reading" or reading with the intent of connecting with God's message on a deeper level while praying for guidance, listening to his voice, and asking for him to transform us.

One of the implications of referring to Jesus as "The Master Teacher" is that we can learn a great deal from examining his life. Throughout this Bible study, our tasks are to discover what Jesus did to earn this title and to determine how we can apply what we learn to our positions as Christian educators. As with any study of Scripture, we must keep in mind that we are not living during Bible times; therefore, we do not know or understand everything about their cultures and customs. Bible commentaries and almanacs enrich our knowledge in this area and add depth to our study. Despite the fact that we cannot literally immerse ourselves in the daily life of that period, we can learn much about how Jesus interacted with people and communicated his message.

Using this Bible Study

The segments of this study are not dependent on previous segments so feel free to pick and choose the order of study. Unless otherwise noted, all Scripture quotations are from the New International Version (NIV). Several segments include multiple Scripture passages and, therefore, may take more than one session to study. Space is provided to record responses within these pages, if desired, or some may wish to keep a separate journal for extended reflection. A red-letter edition of the Bible will quickly identify Jesus' words which might be helpful for some of the segments.

Music: Several of my nieces and nephews would say that I blurt out song lyrics triggered by the current situation. I typically do have music going through my cognitive script, often a hymn. Through singing hymns and choruses of the faith over the years, many deep spiritual truths contained within them were learned or reinforced and retained. As you go through this study, you will find titles of hymns and occasionally contemporary Christian songs that correspond with certain topics. You might enjoy going online, reading the words, or listening to the music as you complete the corresponding segment of the study.

Studying Solo: This Bible study is designed to be flexible; therefore, it may be completed with others or on your own. Some segments contain more Scripture passages than others. When studying alone and with limited time, you may want to either continue the current segment on another day or select just three or four passages from that segment for your focus.

Studying with Others: Because this Bible study is designed for flexibility, it may also be completed with public or private school colleagues before or after school (if permitted), with groups of student teachers, or perhaps with other educators in a small group or special Sunday school class. Whatever the setting, the group may want to agree on which version of the Bible to examine.

When studying with others, the group may decide to go through the study collectively, looking up the Scripture passages and sharing responses orally during the designated meeting time. Or, the group may decide to assign the the next segment as homework each week, focusing discussions during meetings on insights gained during individual study.

Because some segments contain more Scripture passages than others, those segments could be continued to the next session. Or, to use group time efficiently, each person or smaller group may be assigned a different passage to study and then report their findings to the larger group.

Three Perspectives

We will spend most of our time in the four gospels of the New Testament, but we will also look at additional passages and refer to other resources. To organize and guide our study, we will use three words beginning with the letter "i" along with their icons: ***investigate*** (magnifying glass), ***illuminate*** (flashlight), and ***integrate*** (puzzle).

1. To ***investigate***, we will explore the topic as visualized by the magnifying glass. The purpose of this section is to get into the topic, sometimes through background information and other times through Scripture.

2. To ***illuminate***, we will dig deeper into the Bible and other resources to interpret and gain inspiration from specific passages. The flashlight will illuminate our way to "light bulb" ideas, insights, concepts, and principles.

3. To ***integrate***, we will ponder how to incorporate our discoveries into daily classroom situations with the goal of strengthening our teaching. Once all the (puzzle) pieces of our discoveries are in place, we will be better equipped to meet the challenges of teaching.

FAITH MATTERS

CALLED TO TEACH?

"Give of Your Best to the Master"

Educators often wonder if they should leave the profession. I know I have considered it. There are days, weeks, even years, when it appears I am not getting through to students and nothing positive is happening. At those times, I never wanted to be asked, "Why are you a teacher?" as I did not take the question lightly. I have done much prayerful soul searching to determine my rationale for teaching. How would you respond? Beginning teachers as well as veteran educators may find inspiration from reflecting on this question.

Investigate

We begin the investigation by thinking about teaching as a career. What is teaching? Some say teaching is a vocation:

> Your vocation is what you're doing in life that makes a difference. It's something unique to you alone, and it will define your legacy. This is going to be your best vehicle for fulfillment, a sense of peace, and accomplishment. Your vocation is the beacon in your life that keeps you headed in the right direction....[1]

Others say teaching is a calling. What is a calling? A calling can be thought of as God's leading toward something you might describe as your passion. All of your experiences, convictions, abilities, and interests come together, drawing you toward a task that fulfills you on multiple levels and requires you to rely on God's help to achieve and excel.

How do we find our calling? According to pastor and author Dr. John Ortberg, "A calling is something you discover, not something you choose."[2] Ortberg continues by stating, "... our calling is not so much choosing as it is *listening.*"[3] and, "A career is something I choose for myself; a calling is something I receive."[4] Some Christians indicate God called them to places and positions for which they felt inadequate that turn out to be exactly what they needed to stretch them, and they ended up realizing it was perfect for themselves as well as for those they served.

What have you discovered about teaching that leads you to think this is what you should do with your life? How has God led you to become a teacher? Do you feel you are **called** *to teach? If so, how do you know?*

In what meaningful ways does teaching contribute to the Kingdom? How have you affected your students in enduring ways?

In what ways has God enabled you to conquer challenges in teaching? What capacities have you developed due to these challenges?

Illuminate

Continue the investigation by considering your motivation to teach. Teaching is far more than a job or a paycheck because of all the lives you influence in one way or another. Although a love for children is a wonderful motivator, it takes more to be a long-term educator. A favorite teacher may have inspired you to teach, but that is not sufficient motivation. Nor is having a teaching tradition in your family's history. Nor is wanting to help students. Dr. Ortberg comments on those who decide their call based on the needs they see around them.

> It is not hard to figure out where the world's deep need is. It is everywhere! What turns out to be more difficult than you might expect is discovering where your deep gladness lies. What work brings you joy? For what do you have desire and passion—for these, too, are gifts from God.... That does not mean that following a call always brings a feeling of enjoyment. Often it means the gritty resolution to bear with a hard task when it would be easier to quit. But even this yields a certain satisfaction when I know I have been skilled and fitted by God for the task. But I must be ruthlessly honest about *my* deep gladness.[5]

What motivates you to teach? What is the greatest reward or deep gladness you derive from teaching? What specific things about teaching give you a sense of joy, fulfillment, peace, and accomplishment?

Evangelist and author Oswald Chambers cautions us that "… the need is never the call; the need is the opportunity."[6] There will always be a need waiting to be fulfilled, an opportunity for ministry.

Do you want to teach because you perceive the great needs of students? Does Chambers' statement, "The need is never the call…." change your perspective on your motivation to teach? Is it possible to teach effectively out of a burden for the needy rather than due to having a call?

How does God fit into the call? Professor and author Dr. John Van Dyk indicates four ways God equips you to teach: (1) He "endows you with talents," (2) He "provides you with interests," (3) He "equips you for your task by the sort of personality He has bestowed on you" and, (4) He "provides you with opportunities and confronts you with needs."[7]

In comparing yourself to Dr. Van Dyk's list, how well equipped are you to teach?

Integrate

Throughout Scripture God tells us we are created on purpose and for a purpose, and that he has plans for our lives. Read **Jeremiah 29:11** and **Ephesians 2:10**. *What reassurances do you discern related to your current circumstances?*

How would you define your responsibility as a teacher?

How often and in what manner do you pray for your students? Do you pray ***about*** *them rather than* ***for*** *them?*

How committed are you to love your students as Jesus loves you—and loves them? In what ways can you bring characteristics of Jesus into your classroom?

Giant interactive chalkboards, scattered across the United States, invite anyone to complete the statement, "Before I die I want to ______________________." People write about relationships, destinations, dreams, and desires, with the idea that they will work toward fulfilling their goals. Some might compare this to a mission or vision statement. Taking time to think about a calling from this viewpoint enables us to concentrate on the significant things in life and thereby know where to focus our time, talents, and treasures throughout life.

How would you complete this statement?

"Before I die I want to ______________________ for God."

Someone once compared life to a coin. We can spend our coin, our life, on anything, but it is ours to spend just once so we need to make it count. As Christians, our life-long goal should be to spend our lives for God and be able to say as Jesus said, "I have brought you glory on earth by finishing the work you gave me to do" **(John 17:4)**.

When all is said and done, what do you want people to say about your life? What is God leading you to accomplish? How does that fit with your call to teach? As an educator, what do you want to be your legacy? Are your actions and attitudes reflecting your desired legacy?

Summarize your understanding of God's call on your life.

Whatever has gotten you to this point in your life, seek confirmation from God that teaching is what you are supposed to do and then live out that calling **(1 Corinthians 7:17)**. Without that confirmation and without the assurance that God will be with you, teaching can be stressful and discouraging, making it easy to quit. Because God promised to be with us **(Matthew 28:20b)**, teaching can be a joyous adventure. So, ". . . serve him [God] with wholehearted devotion and with a willing mind; for the Lord searches every heart and understands every desire and every thought" **(1 Chronicles 28:9)**.

For further contemplation, you may want to read the writings of Mother Teresa who lived her life in ministry to the poor and helpless. She gives educators much to consider about a relationship with Jesus, selflessness, and sacrifice in working with those on the fringes of society.

FAITH AND LEARNING

"Dare to be a Daniel"

When working in a public institution, Christian educators understand we cannot attempt to convince students to give their lives to God. We also know God is the focus of our lives and teaching is our area of service to him. How can we integrate our faith into the learning process and abide by the law at the same time? How do we reconcile these opposing positions?

Daniel was in a similar situation when he was taken from Israel to serve in the palace of King Nebuchadnezzar. It would have been much easier for him to go along with everything, leave behind his beliefs, and blend in with his new surroundings. Instead, he "… resolved not to defile himself with the royal food and wine, and he asked the chief official for permission not to defile himself this way" **(Daniel 1:8)**. Later, he refused to worship King Darius and "… went home to his upstairs room where the windows opened toward Jerusalem. Three times a day he got down on his knees and prayed, giving thanks to his God, just as he had done before" **(Daniel 6:10).** Throughout all his experiences in a foreign land when others were trying to persuade Daniel to forsake his beliefs, he instead remained true to his convictions, stood up for his faith, and trusted God to protect and provide for him.

Investigate

Just as Daniel was in a position where his faith was put to the test, so Christian educators have their faith tested. How can Christian educators remain true to their beliefs and stand up for their faith in public school settings? Christian educators know they cannot boldly state, "... This is the way, walk in it" **(Isaiah 30:21)**. It is difficult to know what to do or say, or what not do or say. It is much easier to blend in and remain silent. Yet there is a nagging sense that something should be said or done. Someone should stand up for the right; someone should rise up for good, for justice, and for God.

Compare and contrast Daniel's service in a foreign court with service as an educator in your school setting. Creating a T-chart or Venn diagram may help in organizing your ideas.

Illuminate

How can we serve God in public schools when we cannot talk about our doctrine or denomination? Dr. Patricia Clinger, beloved professor and chair of the Division of Education at Bartlesville Wesleyan College for more than 30 years, asked student teachers to consider this situation. She had them respond, in writing, to several questions without using religious terminology. [1]

Follow their lead by replying to the questions in your own words and in writing, as if you were talking to a young child who does not know about God. Your responses are your personal opinions based on your knowledge, background, and experiences related to the Trinity.

1. *Who is God? What do you believe about him? What does he mean to you? What is your relationship to him? How are you connected?*

2. *Who is Jesus? What do you believe about him? What does he mean to you? What is your relationship? How are you connected?*

3. *Who is the Holy Spirit? What do you believe about him? What does he mean to you? What is your relationship? How are you connected?*

Examine your responses. Underline anything you could, as needed, either provide to your students, be to them, or do for them.

Dr. Clinger's fourth question explored God's creativity as shown through his creation—the universe and everything in it:

4. *How can you bring God's creation into the classroom and provide your students with a sense of awe, curiosity, admiration, amazement, and wonder?*

Reponses to the fourth question will vary based on the subjects taught and the instructor. The idea is that by encouraging students to be curious (i.e., be inquisitive about the inner workings of the mind, be astonished at the intricacies of the ecosystem, or be awed over the vastness of the Grand Canyon, etc.), they may begin to consider how it all came about (How did this happen? Whose idea was it? *Who* created it?) and draw the conclusion that it was created intentionally.

Dr. Clinger concluded by indicating that we know we cannot compare ourselves to God. However, we do create our own "world" in the classroom, and by doing the things previously described and underlined, we are bringing some of God's characteristics into our classrooms and "showing his face" to our students. Through us, and with God's help, students can gain a glimpse of how much God loves them.

Spiritual Temperaments. Dr. Gary Thomas, author of *Sacred Pathways,* proposes nine spiritual temperaments or sacred pathways to nurture the soul and reveal our love for God. Several of the pathways include loving God via nature, the senses, the mind, and by loving others.[2] Students display these and other characteristics of their temperaments through their everyday interactions. These temperaments or gifts are God-given and provide avenues for educators to connect with students.

How can we bring various ways of knowing God into the classroom? Are there specific lessons that would benefit from the addition of one or more of these ways to nurture the soul?

Describe students who demonstrate one or more of these spiritual temperaments. How could your instruction enhance their God-given characteristics?

Integrate

Be Kind. How else can we integrate God's characteristics into the classroom? A movement began several years ago to show God's love through random acts of kindness. The basic idea is to do the unexpected or unpleasant and then credit the love of God as the reason for the deed. Some give the waitperson a huge tip or pay for the meal of the next person in the drive through. Others put change in parking meters, open doors, carry packages, give cookies, or leave notes of encouragement. A pastor cleaned restrooms weekly for the restaurant in his small town. All of these kind gestures are intended to demonstrate God's love by being his hands and feet.

Would your students describe you as a kind person? Do they perceive you as caring or uncaring? What acts of kindness do you perform for students in Jesus' name? What opportunities for acts of kindness do you notice at your school?

Holy Spirit. Christians have a momentous way to bring God's characteristics into the classroom, through the Holy Spirit. Jesus promised to provide an advocate, the Holy Spirit, one who would intercede for us, teach us what to say, and provide us wisdom. Read **John 14:26, Luke 12:11-13,** and **John 15:26.** *In what ways do you incorporate these roles of the Holy Spirit into your life and into your position as an educator?*

Be Fruit-Filled. Inviting the Holy Spirit to go with us throughout our day makes a significant difference in the classroom due to the fruit of the Spirit in our lives: "… love, joy, peace, forbearance, kindness, goodness, faithfulness, gentleness and self-control. Against such things there is no law" **(Galatians 5:22-23)**. This list of fruit represents characteristics of those who are filled with the Holy Spirit. With the Holy Spirit guiding our conversation, conduct, and character, our fruit should be prominent in everything we do, say, think, and believe. Demonstrating these characteristics is perfectly legal in any setting **(Galatians 5:23)**.

Which fruit are you permitting the Holy Spirit to display through you? Are any missing? If so, prayerfully consider what changes to make and create a visual reminder to place on a mirror, refrigerator, screen saver, etc.

So, how can we integrate our faith with the learning process? God lives within us. Therefore, we take him and our faith wherever we go, including the classroom. Since God created everything and gives us knowledge and insights into his creation, we humbly thank him and put our minds to the task at hand. We filter what we know and what we learn through the lens of Scripture and our faith. We then apply all of this to assist students in reaching their learning goals.

GRATITUDE

"Give Thanks with a Grateful Heart"

I am convicted by a statement from a wall plaque that reads, "What if you woke up today with only the things you thanked God for yesterday?" I have to ask myself how life would be altered if that were true. Am I genuinely grateful? Have I taken time to thank God for his protection, provision, and providence?" I take for granted things like clean water, electricity, heat and air conditioning, and dependable transportation until something goes wrong. I am typically thankful around Thanksgiving, but it is not always easy to see the "glass half full" the rest of the year. Consistently being grateful and content is challenging.

Investigate

Jesus commented on a lack of thankfulness after healing ten lepers. Read **Luke 17:11-19**. Jesus remarked that only one of the ten thanked him—and the one was not even a Jew. The Samaritan was so grateful that he threw himself at Jesus' feet, an undignified position. Why did the man humble himself like this? Was it because he realized who Jesus was? Was it due to the significance of a Jew healing a Samaritan, someone the Jews considered unworthy? Perhaps it was because healing removed the stigma he experienced from being an untouchable leper **(Leviticus 13)**. Maybe he was just thrilled to be healed.

I wonder about potential implications from this exchange between Jesus and the former leper. Why did the nine neglect to thank Jesus? Why did Jesus comment on that fact? Did he expect to be thanked? Did he want to be thanked? Did the nine take for granted that Jesus would heal them based on what he had done for others? Was Jesus trying to teach a lesson on gratitude to his disciples? *What do you think?*

Illuminate

I often talk with college students about their future lives. I convey that they are young enough to determine their futures by how they decide to go through life. I encourage them to consider their responses to life's adventures and challenges. Will they treat each experience, whether positive or negative, as a learning opportunity? Will they be grateful to God for their experiences? What will they do if life does not turn out the way they thought it would? Will they offer the "sacrifice of praise" **(Hebrews 13:15)** in difficult situations and understand that God uses all experiences for their good **(Romans 8:28)**? Or, will they be like the Israelites in Exodus who complained and grumbled to the point that God called them a "stiff-necked" people and threatened to destroy them? If my students decide to trust God in and through each situation, they will be resilient, grateful, and content no matter the circumstance **(Philippians 4:11)**.

I advise student teachers that the only things under their control in the classroom as well as in life are their responses and their attitudes. They must also recognize the significant influence their inner thoughts have on everything they do and say. "As water reflects the face, so one's life reflects the heart" **(Proverbs 27:19)**. I ask them to consider what they think about and how they think about it. The thoughts of a grateful person are very different from the thoughts of an unappreciative person. Student teachers can let everything upset them, play the blame game, not take responsibility for their actions, and end up realizing that the tragedies in their lives have shaped their identity to the point that they have become bitter. Or, they can resolve within themselves to trust God in all circumstances. I encourage them to grasp the fact that they will not always understand the "whys" or have all the answers, but God can and will turn tragedies into victories. Although Scripture overflows with examples of God creating crowns of beauty from ashes **(Isaiah 61:3)**, it is much easier to speak the words than to live them. I remind them again that the only things any of us control are our responses and attitudes. They make the choice to be either the victims or the victors in the stories of their lives.

The good news is that God tells us how to overcome ingratitude, bitterness, and negative thoughts. A friend likens this to spraying a weed. As the liquid soaks into the leaves, under the skin as it were, it is carried down into the roots where it does the work of killing the weed. Scripture acts like the liquid soaking into us, and it outlines how we can "spray" our negative thoughts to kill the roots of ingratitude and bitterness.

First, we must ask God to reveal any negativity, anger, vindictiveness, or bitterness. "Search me, God, and know my heart; test me and know my anxious thoughts" **(Psalm 139:23)**.

Next, we must permit God to "... take captive every thought...." **(2 Corinthians 10:3-5)** so that we can "... be transformed by the renewing of your mind...." **(Romans 12:2).**

Then, we need to focus on what God recommends: "Finally, brothers and sisters, whatever is true, whatever is noble, whatever is right, whatever is pure, whatever is lovely, whatever is admirable—if anything is excellent or praiseworthy—think about such things" **(Philippians 4:8).** Once God transforms us, we become more resilient by having a grateful heart.

Look up these passages related to gratitude and record your discoveries:

4 Advantages of a Grateful Heart

1. Confidence: **Hebrews 12:28**

2. Joy: **Psalm 94:19, Isaiah 49:13,** and **Psalm 100:1-3**

3. Medicinal Benefits: **Proverbs 17:22**

4. Peace: **Colossians 3:15** and **Philippians 4:4-7**

5 Ways to Demonstrate Gratitude

1. Always, in All Circumstances: **1 Thessalonians 5:16-18**

2. At Church, in Worship: **Psalm 100:4**

3. With Communion: **Luke 22:19b**

4. With Music: **Psalm 69:30, Colossians 3:16,** and **Ephesians 5:18b-19**

5. In Worship: **Hebrews 12:28**

Integrate

People use specific strategies designed to help them have an attitude of gratitude. Ten ideas are provided as thought provokers:

Alphabetical Gratitude. While saying each letter of the alphabet, think of something beginning with that letter for which you are grateful.

Awakening Appreciations. Make it a point to pray when you first awaken in the morning. During this prayer time, think of at least five things for which you are grateful.

Black Hole Focus. At the first meeting with student teachers each semester, I talk about challenges they may face throughout the semester, some seemingly insurmountable. I assure them that I never pray for them to have problems, but I know they will. In fact, if they do not have any difficulties, they are not prepared for their own classrooms. I compare a challenge to a black hole that can eclipse everything else. They can choose to dwell on their problem, let it become all-consuming, and miss what God wants to teach them. Or, they can purposefully choose to focus on the good in their lives. To provide a visual reminder, I give each student teacher a paper with a large black circle in the middle, have them write around the "black hole" how God has blessed them, and then suggest they post the paper someplace where they see it as a daily reminder to be grateful for God's provisions.

Comforting Characteristics. Thank God for his characteristics: his grace, goodness, holiness, love, mercy, power, omnipotence, and wisdom. *What would you add to this list?* We do not deserve anything from God, and we can never sufficiently express our gratitude for his mercies.

Decorations. **Deuteronomy 6:4-9** reveals that God's commands are to be upon our hearts, and we are to teach them to our children, talk of them wherever we go, tie them on our hands, bind them on our foreheads, and write them on our doorposts and gates. One student teacher took this literally and tattooed a verse on his arm. *Are there ways you can express your gratitude to God through your speech as well as your decorations at home and in your classroom?*

Grateful Hands. At the end of the semester, I have student teachers create a visual reminder of people who helped them throughout their student teaching experience. Using the outline of their hand, they write within each digit the name of someone who made a significant contribution to their success. They are encouraged to express gratitude to these five people as well as others who supported them during their semester of student teaching.

Gratitude Baggies. A few years ago, students raised money to support needy children by distributing baggies to collect monetary contributions. In each baggie was an outline of the dates between Thanksgiving and Christmas break with the name of an object and a corresponding amount. For example, on the first date you were to donate five cents for every shoe you owned. Other items on the list included pillows, t-shirts, balls, hair products, etc. Not only did this activity raise money, it also raised awareness of our blessings and the needs of others.

Journaling. A friend keeps a gratitude journal by daily recording the good things that happen. She stated that looking back at the blessings recorded in her journal and searching for something good to write about every day kept her going after the unexpected death of her husband.

Memorials. Several times when God did momentous things for the Israelites, they created memorials (typically stacked rocks) as visual reminders **(Joshua 4:3-7)**. When children asked the meaning of the memorials, their elders recounted stories of God's protection and provision. *Perhaps you would not stack rocks in the midst of your yard, but what visual could you use as a reminder for yourself of God's care that could also act as a teaching tool for children?* Perhaps it is a cross dangling from your rear-view mirror. Perhaps, as in my case, it is a quilt given to our family in a time of need.

Songs in the Night. When I am half awake at night, a song of worship and praise is often running through my mind. It is usually something we were practicing at church, either in the adult or children's choirs. Singing dispels my negative or worrisome thoughts and is a way to express my gratitude to God.

What other ideas would you add to the list of ways to express gratitude? Are there any strategies you could do yourself, do together with your students, or encourage your students to do for themselves?

A grateful heart leads to the kind of contentment Paul talks about in **Philippians 4:11b-12**. *How will you maintain a grateful heart, that attitude of gratitude, while traversing the mountains and valleys of life?*

LIGHT OF THE WORLD

"This Little Light of Mine"

The concept of "light" is fascinating to me, yet I take for granted that I can "create" light by flipping a switch. Light not only illuminates the room, it is a necessary part of the lifecycle and vital for our continued existence. Plants need light to survive and we depend on plants for food as well as for the oxygen they provide. Light performs many functions.

I think of times when "light" played a significant role in a darkened worship setting as one person lit a candle and used it to pass along the light to others until the entire space was bright. I also think of the significance of even a small flashlight on midnight hikes at youth camp in the Bradshaw Mountains of Arizona. I have witnessed light creating stunning sunrises and sunsets over the Grand Canyon where we often vacationed as a family. Standing on the South Rim of the Canyon after dark, we could see light from the North Rim, some ten miles away.

When I was quite young, our family toured Carlsbad Caverns in New Mexico. I was impressed by the immense stalactites reaching down and stalagmites growing up (facts I learned during our tour). I recall thinking it was odd to find a cafeteria in the cavern. However, what I remember the most is what happened after they turned out the lights. Although forewarned, the deep darkness engulfed everything and felt suffocating. I could not see anyone, not even those standing beside me. Had I not been holding Mom's hand, I may have cried out.

Investigate

Of the statements Jesus make about himself, "light" is the only one he indicated we are. Read **Matthew 6:14-16**. *What did Jesus mean when he said we are the light of the world? As you read the below passages, record the references to light.*

- **2 Samuel 23:2-4**
- **Psalm 27:1**
- **Psalm 119:105**
- **Isaiah 42:16**
- **Isaiah 58:8**
- **Matthew 5:14-16**
- **John 1:6-9**
- **John 3:19-21**
- **John 8:12**
- **Ephesians 5:8-14**

Illuminate

Study your list to determine what light should be and do. What qualities does it have?

What do you notice about God and Jesus in these passages?

Compare your findings about light to what Professor Steve Hughes shared in a Sunday School presentation at First Wesleyan Church, Bartlesville, Oklahoma. According to the outline offered by Hughes, light does three things:

1. Light comes out of the darkness. A single, tiny light dispels the darkness.
   (I would add that light is brightest in the deepest darkness.)
   a. Despair vs. Hope
   b. Lost vs. Found
   c. Helplessness vs. Purposefulness
2. Light comes in spite of the darkness.
   a. Darkness may be overwhelming and foreboding—think "good vs. evil"
   b. Darkness may try to stop the light by intimidation and fear
3. Light changes the darkness.[1]

Integrate

There are those who say Christians should not teach in public schools. In talking to them, I typically describe Christian educators as lights and ask them what would happen if all these lights were removed from the public education system. *What are your thoughts about this?*

Many people today live in a world filled with suffocating darkness. There are children who grow up not knowing anything else. Jesus said he is the light of the world and also that we are to be light by permitting him to shine in us and through us.

What does it mean to let your light shine before others? How can you display "light" in your classroom? What can you do to be a lighthouse for Jesus, glorifying your heavenly father?

How can you "hold hands" with your students and help dispel the suffocating presence of darkness in their lives? How can you instill hopefulness and purposefulness in your students?

MADE IN HIS IMAGE

"I Belong to the King"

We hear a lot about products "made in the USA" with the implication that their quality is better than the quality of products made elsewhere. There is a line "products" of the highest quality, made for thousands of years, each "product" having unique characteristics. You may have guessed that YOU are one of these creations and that God is the creator. Let's investigate the implications of being made in the image of God (**Genesis 1:27**).

Investigate

As you read the passages, consider the creativity and careful design God displays through his creations which are made in the Imago Dei (Latin for *image of God*). Reflect on all the complex systems, intricate organs, and microscopic facets that have to work together perfectly for humans to be created, survive, and thrive. Record your thoughts.

- **Genesis 1:26-31**

- **Isaiah 44:24**

- **1 Corinthians 11:7b**

- **Psalm 139** (especially verses 13-16)

Illuminate

Items produced assembly-line style are identical. Human beings are not identical. What does it mean to be unique? There are multiple physical features used to identify a distinct individual: fingerprint, voice pattern, and eye scan to name a few. Each physical feature (such as a fingerprint) has characteristics unique to just one individual throughout history. Consider other human dimensions that create further uniqueness: intellectual, spiritual, emotional, social, experiential, personality, temperament, motivation, attitude, culture, background, etc. It is overwhelming to think that each of these physical features and dimensions reveal a combination of characteristics that are unique to just one person. Author Dr. Kathy Koch, founder and president of Celebrate Kids, Inc., asserts that we are "... unrepeatable miracles of God.[1] Unrepeatable. Never-to-be-repeated in the history of the world. The one and only. Nobody else will be identical, ever! We truly are miracles, created by God, and created in the image of God.

It is impossible to adequately express the limitless creativity of God in creating us. David had it right when he said we are "... fearfully and wonderfully made" **(Psalm 139:14)**. It is also impossible to adequately express the love God has for his creation. He must really love us to go to all that effort to create each of us so uniquely.

What are the implications for educators? What should be our foundational perspectives? As you consider this brief list, think about what you would add.

- Each student is made in God's image; therefore, each student displays clues into God's characteristics **(Genesis 1:27).**
- Each student is to be valued as a unique, never-to-be-repeated creation of God **(Luke 12:24).**
- Each student is to be treated as irreplaceable **(Ephesians 1:4-5).**
- Each student is created by God for a purpose **(Ephesians 2:10).**
- Each student should be considered an assignment from God.

Integrate

Focus either on one student or an entire class as you reflect on your students as God's Image Bearers.

Image Bearers. *What characteristics of God are displayed through your student(s)? In what ways do you perceive God through your student(s)?*

Unique and Irreplaceable. *What unique and irreplaceable characteristics do you detect in your student(s), positive or negative?* You may want to consider a variety of dimensions such as their backgrounds, experiences, family support, world viewpoints, intellectual capacity, knowledge base, learning characteristics, strengths and weaknesses, likes and dislikes, personality traits, temperaments, attitudes, etc.

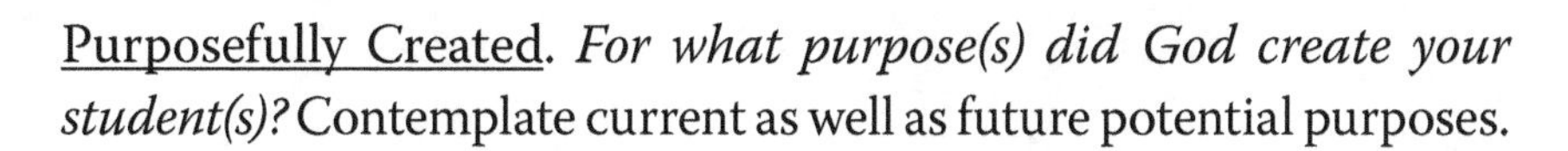

Purposefully Created. *For what purpose(s) did God create your student(s)?* Contemplate current as well as future potential purposes.

Assignment from God. *What is your assignment from God via your student(s)? Why do you think God put this student or combination of students in your class? What are you supposed to learn from your student(s)? What are you supposed to do for your student(s)? What will you never forget about your student(s)?*

Impact. Since each student is unique and irreplaceable, created by God for a purpose, and placed in your class as an assignment from God, *how do these facts impact your interactions and relationships?*

What insights do you glean from viewing students through God's eyes? How can you apply your insights? What should you change, intentionally do, avoid doing, or keep in mind?

PRAYER

"Sweet Hour of Prayer"
"Whisper a Prayer"

Every educator in a public school in the United States knows that the law says you cannot pray in school, aloud that is. You may have heard a humorous statement along the lines that there will always be prayer in school as long as there are tests. No matter how the legal system attempts to separate church and school, as long as God is moving in human hearts, there will be prayer in school, at least silent prayer.

Investigate

Many students know the value of prayer and, although personal beliefs are not discussed in school, they know which teachers believe in prayer. They know who they can ask to pray for their burdens. They come to this knowledge from observing and interacting with these teachers who live out their faith moment by moment by being the hands, feet, and heart of Jesus. Students listen to their teachers' responses to complex questions, they see how teachers react in stressful situations, they note how they treat struggling or defiant students, they witness deeds of compassion, and they watch to learn if teachers are consistent in maintaining their beliefs.

Christian educators can share many examples about the power of praying for students and colleagues. Although I could describe many personal experiences, I offer one from a friend, a middle school teacher. She revealed that every morning she stands behind each desk, praying for all the students who will sit there throughout the day. One morning a student arrived early and, as she entered the classroom, asked if my teacher friend could see the angel standing behind her desk. What a powerful demonstration of God's watch-care over these students and answer to my friend's prayer!

What answers to prayer for students or colleagues have you had?

Illuminate

The Lord's Prayer. I do not claim to know everything there is to know about prayer. There are a multitude of resources for those interested in an extensive study. However, Jesus provided an example of how to pray with The Lord's Prayer. Read **Matthew 6:1-15**. *What do you notice in comparing **Matthew 6:1-8** with your situation and school setting?*

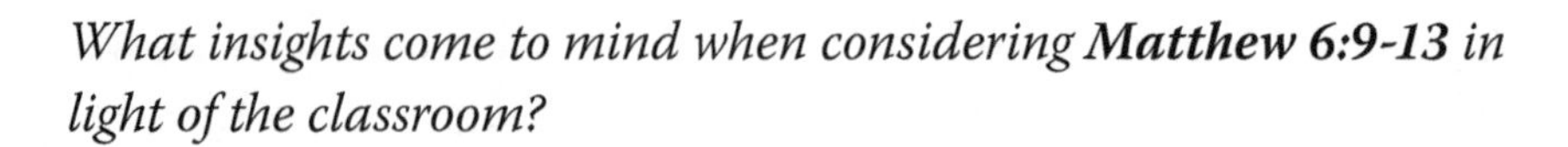

What insights come to mind when considering ***Matthew 6:9-13*** *in light of the classroom?*

What role does forgiveness, as articulated in ***Matthew 6:14-15,*** *play in your relationships with students and colleagues?*

<u>The High Priestly Prayer</u>. Jesus provided another example of how to pray in what is commonly called The High Priestly Prayer. Read **John 17:1-26**. *Which statements can be applied to educators or students?* Create a list.

Integrate

How can you apply The Lord's Prayer ***(Matthew 6:1-15)*** *in talking with God about your students?*

Drawing on statements from The High Priestly Prayer ***(John 17:1-26)****, write an educator's prayer and use it frequently.*

Praying for Students. Author Bob Hostetler created an app and a bookmark, "31 Ways to Pray for Your Kids," which provides an intentional prayer strategy to ask God to help children grow in biblical characteristics, one trait per day.[1] Think about the power of praying for each of your students to cultivate a different godly characteristic each day. Priceless!

Along the same line of praying for the attainment of one attribute a day, some educators pray for their students to develop the fruits of the Spirit (**Galatians 5:22-23**).

SALT

"Salt and Light"

Jesus begins the Sermon on the Mount with the Beatitudes and then, curiously, says we are two things, one of which is salt. Salt is one of those things we do not really think about until it is missing. The word itself is used in a variety of ways. We often hear phrases related to salt: "She's the salt of the earth." or "Don't rub salt into the wound." We are admonished to "take it with a grain of salt" and we go "back to the salt mines" on Monday mornings. We sprinkle the word "salt" throughout our conversations and on our meals. What did Jesus mean when he said we are the salt of the earth?

Investigate

As you inspect these passages, create a list of characteristics and concepts related to salt. What qualities does salt have?

- **Matthew 5:13**
- **Mark 9:49-50**
- **Colossians 4:6**
- **James 3:10-12**

Scripture records a "covenant of salt" in three places. Read **Leviticus 2:13, Numbers 18:19,** and **2 Chronicles 13:5**. A covenant was the most sacred, permanent, and unchangeable agreement. The covenant of salt

> ... signified the purity and persevering fidelity that were necessary in the worship of God. Everything was seasoned with it, to signify the purity and perfection that should be extended through every part of the divine service and through the hearts and lives of God's worshippers. It was called the salt of the covenant of thy (Abram's) God, because as salt is incorruptible, so was the covenant made with Abram,....[1]

From your list and Scripture readings, what should salt be and do? How is it used?

Illuminate

According to *Salt, the Fifth Element,* salt has several qualities: it seasons (adds flavor), preserves (hinders decay; dehydrates and cures food), purifies (cleanses wounds; promotes healing), soothes (alleviates pain and soreness of the throat, feet, etc.), melts (thaws the frozen ice and snow), and softens (makes water palatable).[2]

> Salt was a commodity of great value in the biblical world. It was recognized as essential to life and was used in the preservation of food, as a purifying agent and antiseptic against corruption and decay,

> as a seasoning, and even as a fertilizer for certain types of plants and soil. In earlier times, soldiers received their wages (*sal*ary) in salt; covenants were made based on salt; and major trade routes were established for the exchange of salt.[3]

Although it has many positive characteristics, salt can also be harmful, especially if used excessively. Salt can be abrasive, it can ruin flavor, it can harm health, it can rust, or it can destroy.

Integrate

Are there any incorruptible, sacred, permanent, or unchangeable covenants in your classroom?

Describe classroom examples of seasoning, preserving, purifying, soothing, melting, and softening. How else might characteristics of salt correlate to the classroom?

How can the negative qualities of salt, such as corrosion or abrasiveness, be avoided in the classroom?

How do you exhibit "salt" in your life and classroom? How can you be a salt shaker for Jesus?

SEED SOWERS

"Bringing in the Sheaves"

You are familiar with THAT student. The one who is so challenging that you are exhausted before noon. Through the years, I have tried to teach several versions of that student (emphasis on tried), but the one who stands out the most was a high school student everyone was afraid of, including me. I still shudder inside when I think of him because I could see pure evil in his eyes. All kinds of unusual things happened to me that year: broken windows, excrement in the classroom, and slashed tires to name a few. While these examples appear mild compared to some of the tragedies in schools today, it was quite a stressful year for me.

I knew I was called to teach and this was where God wanted me. I also knew I was not affecting THAT student, and I was very discouraged by my inability to reach him. However, I prayed a lot, went to school every day, and persisted in my attempts to connect with him in some way. I admit that many of my efforts were halfhearted. I wondered if it was possible to make a difference in his life and knew that God would have to intervene for that to happen.

Investigate

Read about the farmer in the parable Jesus told as found in **Matthew 13:1-9.**

What do you notice about how the farmer performed the task of sowing seeds?

What do you notice about the soil? Did the type of soil matter to the farmer's spreading of seeds?

What experiences have you had with various types of soil when sowing seeds of God's love to your students?

Grit. Several recent books address the character trait of grit, alluding to the fact that the best teachers (and students) have this trait. Grit encompasses several character traits like persistence, resilience, and willpower that enable educators to stick with long-term tasks such as connecting with struggling students.

What is the relationship between sowing seeds and the characteristics of faithfulness, resilience, persistence, and willpower?

How does an educator's grit connect with sowing seeds of God's love? What other qualities of grit would benefit an educator?

Illuminate

THAT student had the hardest soil in my teaching experience. Even though I was aware of some horrendous things in this student's background and endeavored to form a relationship, nothing I did appeared to have any kind of effect. I completely related to the statement when Jesus said he was ". . . sending you out like sheep among wolves.... Be on your guard" **(Matthew 10:16-17a).** I certainly felt vulnerable that year, like a sheep being trailed by a wolf, and always on my guard. Throughout that entire school year, I had no indication of any kind of change in THAT student and it was very easy for me to worry and be fearful.

How does one sow seeds of God's love while being on your guard at the same time?

Have you experienced a circumstance during which it was much easier to worry than to trust God?

Jesus continued in **Matthew 10:19b-20** with a directive and promise: ". . . do not worry about what to say or how to say it. At that time, you will be given what to say, for it will not be you speaking, but the Spirit of your Father speaking through you."

What experience have you had of the Holy Spirit speaking through you as an educator?

Integrate

Many educators have had a student recount something they said or did that made a difference in the student's life. When that has happened to me, it usually was not anything big or special, and I may not remember the specific incident. In these instances, I have concluded that God prepared the student's soil, worked through me as I sowed seeds, and nurtured the seed (perhaps through others) so it had the opportunity to take root and grow.

I realized the power of sowing seeds when, at the end of that very long school year, the counselor told me this challenging student had confided to him that I was his favorite teacher. I was so unprepared for this news that my mind could not comprehend it for a moment. The counselor wanted to know how I became his favorite. The only thing I could think of was that I prayed—a lot! I later realized the Holy Spirit was working and speaking through me, and I was unknowingly planting small seeds.

Has a student conveyed something you said or did that made a difference to him or her? Did you remember the circumstance described? Was it something extraordinary? Was it something you habitually say or do?

Make a list of the kinds of things you consider to be sowing seeds of God's love in your students.

Compare your list with the lists of other educators. Are there additional things you could do or say that might make a difference in the lives of your students?

Even on days when there is no thought that our duties and responsibilities as educators are in any way contributing to the Kingdom, our job is to ". . . be faithful with a few things...." **(Matthew 25:23b)** by sowing the seeds of God's love far and wide with faith, knowing that God will prepare the soil and the seeds will take root in his timing.

INSTRUCTIONAL STRATEGIES FROM THE MASTER

ASSESSMENT

"We'll Understand It Better By and By"

The emphasis on assessment exploded in the USA with the enactment of "No Child Left Behind" in 2002. Due to the shift in government requirements, curriculum changed, as did the focus of curriculum, which now centers on improving student achievement. Testing aside, assessment's ultimate goal is to determine what is going on inside. What do students know and understand in their heads and hearts? What can students do with their hands? Because we cannot know what is going on inside (what is in their hearts) educators have developed multiple ways to measure or assess knowledge (what is in their heads) and what they can do (with their hands).

You may have heard the phrase, "Begin with the end in mind," one of Stephen Covey's habits for highly effective people.[1] To be effective, we must know the end goal or objective. At the end of instruction, what should students know, understand, or be able to do? Everything done in the classroom revolves around the objective. Once the objective (the end goal) is determined, we work backwards to establish how to attain it.

Two terms, formative and summative, are used to describe categories of assessment. Formative assessment focuses on how students are doing as they are in the process of learning. During instruction, teachers monitor student progress by obtaining feedback and data through a variety of strategies which inform their next steps. Based on the results of these formative assessment strategies, teachers determine whether or not students are working toward achievement of the objective. If so, they keep moving forward. If not, they adjust instruction by re-teaching, remediating, or employing other strategies to communicate the information.

Summative assessment occurs at the end of the unit's instruction. It informs teachers about their students' attainment of the objective once the unit is finished. Findings from the summative assessment are used to improve student learning, the bottom line for implementing both formative and summative assessment strategies.

Investigate

Scripture does not use terms like formative and summative assessment. However, can we find examples of assessment used by Jesus? If so, what did Jesus want to accomplish in and through his disciples, and how did he know if he was successful? How did Jesus begin with the end in mind? *Describe your perceptions of the goals Jesus wanted to accomplish while on earth. In other words, what were his objectives? Create a list.*

As you read the listed passages, record your responses to two questions:

1. *What was Jesus trying to teach and communicate in these situations?*

2. *How would you classify the type of "assessment" Jesus used in these situations?* Some potential assessment terms might include authentic, diagnostic, formative, guided, objective, subjective, and summative. Perhaps you would add other terms. While considering the passages, you might use more than one term for the specific situation.

- **Matthew 10:1-42**–Disciples sent 2 x 2

- **Luke 10:1-24**–72 sent

- **Matthew 16:13-20** and **Luke 9:18-27**–Who do people say I am?

- **Mark 6:30-44**–You feed them

- **John 9:35-41**–Spiritual blindness

- **Luke 9:28-36**–Mount of Transfiguration

- **John 16:25-32**–Figurative speaking

- **Matthew 26:36-46**–Garden of Gethsemane

Illuminate

Much of what Jesus did in training his followers could be classified as formative assessment. He implemented many ways to determine the progress made by his students. Referring back to the Scripture passages, *how did Jesus involve his students? What strategies did he use?*

In what ways did Jesus monitor progress and use feedback to improve student learning? How was he keeping the end in mind?

Consult your list of Jesus' objectives. *How successful do think he was in accomplishing these objectives?*

It is easy to say Jesus was always successful because of who he is and the fact that his message has persisted and transformed lives for more than 2,000 years. It is also easy to compare our own shortcomings and then become discouraged.

Read this sampling of passages from Mark for insights into how people responded to Jesus' message and actions. Record your findings.

- **Mark 9:32**

- **Mark 5:14-15**

- **Mark 10:32**

- **Mark 11:18**

- **Mark 3:5**

- **Mark 6:6**

- **Mark 9:19**

If time permits, scan one of the four gospels to determine how often Jesus had to "re-teach" concepts like heaven and his death.

Do you think his followers truly "got it" before he died? Did they understand after he ascended to heaven?

We can never categorize Jesus as unsuccessful, but Scripture does provide clues indicating that his ideas were very distinct and challenging. Therefore, not everyone was willing to believe and receive him. One of his chosen disciples, Judas, failed the ultimate test (the final) and betrayed him in spite of all the instruction, interactions, prayer, and time Jesus poured into his life. This should encourage us, as educators, to understand that we may not be able to succeed with every student. It does not mean that we give up on any student, but it helps us recognize that each person makes choices with which we may not agree. We can instruct, encourage, and advise, but ultimately, we cannot control what students do. We do our part and give God our burden for our students.

Integrate

How do we know if our instruction has succeeded? How do we assess our students? Jesus has an advantage over us in that he knows each person's inner motives and heart desires **(Psalm 139:1-4)**. Because we cannot know our students to that depth, we have to depend on the outward—what they know, understand, or can do. We can see how they progress as student scholars. It may take years to learn how well a student does in life. Some educators may be fortunate enough to hear back from former students. However, we may never know what happens to many students. God never guarantees our success. He does ask us to be faithful to our calling and trust his plan for our students.

In Jesus' High Priestly Prayer, we find what might be classified as self-assessment when Jesus says, "I have brought you glory on earth by finishing the work you gave me to do" **(John 17:4)**. Jesus considered his task accomplished, even if not everyone accepted him.

What other examples of self-assessment do you find in the High Priestly Prayer **(John 17:1-26)**? *Do any relate to your teaching?*

Are you bringing God glory on earth? Are you faithfully seeking his leadership each day, applying Scripture to current situations, praying for and serving your students? Are you obeying the Holy Spirit's direction (formative assessment)? If so, you can confidentially leave the results (summative assessment) to God.

CONVERSATIONS WITH JESUS

"He Walks with Me"

Have you ever considered instruction as an extended conversation with students? For many students, teachers are the ones with whom they have the longest conversations on any given day. Jesus had numerous conversations with people (his students) from a variety of backgrounds, and he used many methods to capture their interest and convey his point.

Investigate

Read the passages featuring conversations with Jesus and then respond to the questions which are adapted from *Teaching as Jesus Taught* by Dr. Roy B. Zuck,[1] authoritative author and senior professor at Dallas Theological Seminary, who provides a variety of perspectives related to four of Jesus' conversations recorded in Scripture.

- **Matthew 19:16-22**–the rich young man

- **Luke 7:36-47**–the Pharisee

- **John 3:1-21**–Nicodemus

- **John 9:1, 6-7, & 35-39**–the blind man

How did Jesus interest these "students" in learning?

What were their initial responses to Jesus?

What did Jesus say or do after the initial interactions?

What were the students' final responses to Jesus (if recorded)? Were the outcomes positive or negative?

Illuminate

Refer back to the Scripture passages as you respond.

How did Jesus use questions or statements to communicate with people?

Did Jesus answer their questions directly or indirectly? Which questions were direct? Which were indirect?

Who asked more questions—Jesus or the people to whom he was talking?

How did Jesus vary his approach to each individual?

How did Jesus ensure that each one got the point—the reality of who he was and is?

If you were to classify his statements or questions according to difficulty levels, what kinds of thinking were required to respond? Were Jesus' statements or questions primarily factual or did they have to apply, analyze, or synthesize information?

How would you describe (in educational terminology) what Jesus did and how he handled the situations? What personal qualities did he display?

Integrate

Make a list of what you learned about how Jesus conversed with his "students" in various situations. What methods did Jesus employ? How do these methods relate to conversations in your classroom?

JESUS, THE MASTER TEACHER

"My Jesus (Teacher)"

Why is Jesus referred to as The Master Teacher? What is it about his teaching that has captivated people for centuries? Perhaps it is the way he communicated and related to people. Perhaps it is because his message is still relevant and has the power to change lives. Perhaps it is because he provides a model of teaching to which we can aspire.

Scripture records people calling Jesus teacher or rabbi over and over. In the Jewish tradition, rabbis were respected and considered authorities on the Old Testament, the Bible available during this time. These rabbis would seek the most promising young scholars to be their students. How do we know Jesus' instruction was different from other rabbis? Scripture tells us, "The people were amazed at his teaching, because he taught them as one who had authority, not as the teachers of the law" **(Mark 1:22)**. His authority, knowledge of Scripture, and interpretation of Scripture were some of the characteristics that set him apart from other rabbis. We might say that the rabbis had head knowledge. Jesus had head knowledge as well as heart and experiential knowledge.

Investigate

While it is difficult to translate everything Jesus did into today's culture and classrooms, we can make some comparisons that will help us understand more about his role as teacher. Survey your choice of one of the four gospels and use educational terms to respond to the questions by listing the reference and your responses. A red-letter edition of the Bible will quickly identify Jesus' words.

What were Jesus' main activities? How would you use educational terms to categorize what he did? (i.e., teaching...)

What types of teaching did Jesus do? What teaching strategies did he use?

How would you categorize the examples and illustrations Jesus used?

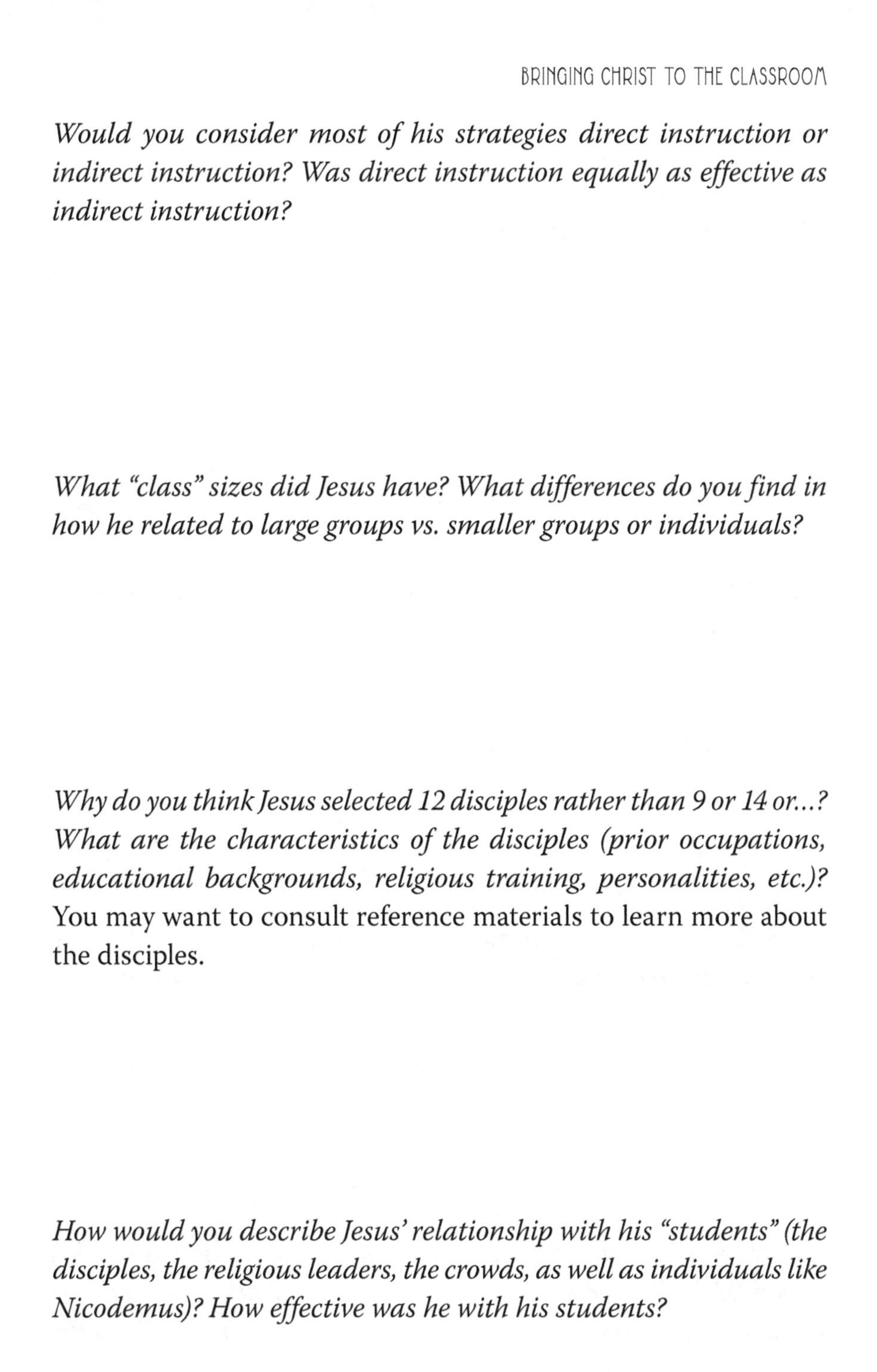

Would you consider most of his strategies direct instruction or indirect instruction? Was direct instruction equally as effective as indirect instruction?

What "class" sizes did Jesus have? What differences do you find in how he related to large groups vs. smaller groups or individuals?

Why do you think Jesus selected 12 disciples rather than 9 or 14 or...? What are the characteristics of the disciples (prior occupations, educational backgrounds, religious training, personalities, etc.)? You may want to consult reference materials to learn more about the disciples.

How would you describe Jesus' relationship with his "students" (the disciples, the religious leaders, the crowds, as well as individuals like Nicodemus)? How effective was he with his students?

Illuminate

Why do you think Jesus used the teaching strategies, examples, illustrations, etc., you discovered in your investigation? What was he trying to achieve?

Did Jesus use what we would refer to as "best practices" for his time and culture? If so, what were some of these practices? Could these practices be used today?

How did Jesus cultivate relationships with his "students" (the disciples, the religious leaders, the crowds, and individuals)?

Did Jesus tailor his instruction based on characteristics of his students? Did he have relationships with students who would be considered challenging in some way? What do you notice about the strategies he used to interact with his students?

Integrate

Our goal should be to look at Scripture through the eyes of an educator to glean strategies and ideas that we can employ in our classrooms and in our relationships with students.

Can we teach today like Jesus did in his time? Which of Jesus' strategies can we implement?

How can our teaching have long-term influence on our students, similar to the impact Jesus' teaching had on his students?

METAPHORS

"The Love of God"

Jesus used language as a communication tool. Rather than bluntly stating something that would soon be forgotten, he used many figures of speech to communicate with those around him. The metaphor, simile, paradox, and irony were often used to make a point, help people see things in a different manner, and enable them to understand more rapidly.

Metaphors are commonplace in our conversations: we come to a "fork in the road," we "learn the ropes" in a new position, we "stand on the shoulders of giants," or it is "raining cats and dogs" outside. Metaphors become part of us because we hear their repeated use by family and others around us. We use them because they help us compare and describe things in more interesting ways.

In relating why Jesus used metaphors, Dr. Roy B. Zuck, authoritative author of *Teaching as Jesus Taught* and senior professor at Dallas Theological Seminary, says, "The metaphor presented a literal truth figuratively and thus it arrests our *attention*, challenges us to *think*..., and is easier to *recall*" (italics added).[1] In other words, the Master Teacher used figures of speech, like metaphors, to:

1. make what he said ***relevant***,
2. encourage us to ***reflect*** on the meaning, and
3. make it easier for us to ***retain*** what we learned.

Investigate

Consider the effectiveness of the metaphors Jesus used by reviewing four examples. After reading each passage, describe:

1. *Was the metaphor **relevant** to those hearing it then? To us today?*
2. *How are we encouraged to **reflect** on the meaning of the metaphor?*
    a. *What can we learn from the metaphor? What is implied?*
    b. *What (if any) connections are there between the metaphor and teaching?*
3. *Why is it easier for us to **retain** what we learned about the metaphor?*

- **Matthew 5:13-16**
    - Relevant
    - Reflect
    - Retain
- **Matthew 13:1-9**
    - Relevant
    - Reflect
    - Retain
- **John 10:1-18**
    - Relevant

  - o Reflect
  - o Retain

- **John 15:1-8**
  - o Relevant
  - o Reflect
  - o Retain

Illuminate

Many authors discuss the use of metaphors in gaining unique perspectives on puzzling situations. These perspectives bring new insights, inspiration, and unexpected solutions. *Think quickly—what metaphor would you use to describe yourself as an educator? Give it a title.* For example, the title of my metaphor is Lacemaker.

Elaborate on your metaphor.

For example, lacemakers do a lot of planning prior to executing a lace pattern which equates to the research, decisions, and preparation that go into lesson planning. These are things my metaphor has in common with teaching. My metaphor differs from teaching in that the end product, the lace, conforms to the pattern. Each student is unique. They do not always conform to expectations. My metaphor would compare and contrast other significant aspects of teaching with those of making lace.

How does your metaphor compare? Create a Venn diagram or T-chart of descriptive words and phrases comparing and contrasting the tasks of educators with how your metaphor works or what it does.

What similarities between your metaphor and teaching do you discover that would otherwise be overlooked? How is your metaphor not like teaching?

What strengths and weaknesses do you detect in your metaphor? How might these influence your teaching?

Integrate

Describe a specific situation when you knew things could have gone better, but you were not sure what you should have done. Use your teaching metaphor to think through the situation. What guidance does your metaphor provide? How might your metaphor influence your future perceptions, priorities, and expectations?

Reflect on a lesson in which you use a metaphor as an instructional strategy. How is the metaphor ***relevant*** *to your students? How do you encourage them to* ***reflect*** *on the meaning and applications of the metaphor? Is it easy for students to* ***retain*** *what they learned due to the metaphor? Is the metaphor an effective strategy to use in your lesson?*

What other lesson topics or concepts would benefit from the use of metaphors?

PARABLES

"Parable Song"

Jesus was an expert in using stories and figures of speech to communicate with those around him. We often think of the parable as one of the main strategies Jesus used to convey his message. In fact, Jesus is so closely associated with parables that after a search for the word "parables" on the Internet, you will see part of the definition often includes Jesus, and his parables are frequently used as examples.

A parable is simply a story, often with a surprising twist, that carries a message or something to consider. It is interesting to note that most of the parables Jesus told focus on humans in familiar situations. In other words, the parables were very relevant to those listening to Jesus. Jesus often used parables as a means of addressing controversial issues. The listeners understood the everyday circumstances and settings involved in the stories, yet the metaphor provided new things to ponder.

Investigate

Read **Matthew 13:10-17** and **10:35**. *Paraphrase the rationale Jesus gave for using parables.*

Describe the characteristics of those Jesus said would understand his parables vs. those who would not understand them. How closely related are these characteristics to those of your students?

In addition to the rationale Jesus described, he used parables for at least three other reasons pertinent to educators:

1. To make what he said ***relevant*** to his listeners at the time—and to us now
2. To encourage us to ***reflect*** on the meaning
3. To make it easier to ***retain*** what we learned

Would you add any other reasons to this list?

Analyze some of the parables recorded in Matthew to determine their underlying message(s). *What everyday situations did Jesus use to make the parables **relevant** to his listeners? In what ways was **reflection** required? Describe some of the **reactions** to these parables. How were the messages of the parables received? Were the messages **retained**?*

- **Matthew 7:24-29**–Building on Rock or Sand

- **Matthew 9:14-17**–Wedding; Garment; Wine

- **Matthew 13:31-35** and **44-52**–Kingdom of Heaven

- **Matthew 18:23-35**–Settling of Accounts

- **Matthew 20:1-16**–Hired Laborers

- **Matthew 21:28-46**–Repentant Son; Murderous Tenants

- **Matthew 22:1-15**–Marriage Feast

- **Matthew 25:1-30**–Waiting for the Bridegroom; Settling of Accounts

For further study, search one of the other gospels for additional parables used by Jesus.

Illuminate

How would you classify parables as a teaching strategy? (Are parables student or teacher centered? Are they a direct or an indirect instructional strategy?)

What teaching principles could parables illustrate? For example, going from the known to the unknown, concrete to abstract, etc. What level of thinking would be required to understand the depth of parables? Would all of your students be able to achieve that level of understanding?

Describe a parable (story) you have used to introduce or illustrate a concept. Was the story ***relevant*** *to your students? Did it encourage them to* ***reflect*** *on the concept? How were students enabled to* ***retain*** *the concept? Would you say the story was successful? If not, how might you improve it?*

The use of parables—relevant, fascinating stories, often with a surprising twist—is a powerful strategy for enticing students to think. *What tips would you give a beginning storyteller who is attempting to make parables relevant, understandable, challenging, and memorable?*

Are there concepts your students struggle to understand? If so, search for parables that would introduce or illustrate the concepts and consider these questions before inserting the stories into the lessons:

1. *What everyday situations could you use to make the concepts **relevant** to your students?*

2. *What **surprising elements** could you include? How could you **inspire the imaginations** of your students? How could you make the stories **memorable**?*

3. *How could you use the stories to encourage your students to **reflect** on the concepts?*

4. *In what ways would the stories help your students **retain** the concepts?*

PREPARATION FOR TEACHING

"Prepare the Way"

"Proper preparation prevents poor performance."
(Attributed to multiple sources)

There are those who enjoy preparing for something—an event, a vacation, a new process, etc. They make lists, they organize materials, and they create tools to make tasks easier. Although you cannot tell it by looking at my desk, I am one of those who feels off balance if I am not organized.

Proper preparation is emphasized throughout the teacher training process because the success of the lesson depends on it. Good teachers have many things to consider before, during, and after instruction. Some of these things include:

1. Knowing what their boss (principal, superintendent, and school board) expects of them.
2. Knowing what they need to accomplish related to the instructional subject (a.k.a., the objectives).
3. Knowing their students well enough to know their strengths and weaknesses, their likes and dislikes, and their preferred ways of learning.
4. Knowing their subject(s).

5. Knowing how to assess the objectives and determine if they have been successfully achieved.
6. Knowing how to use the results of assessments to improve both student learning and instruction.

Investigate

Scripture provides some parallels in the life of Jesus to these instructional considerations. Think about Jesus as the Master Teacher. *How did Jesus prepare for his ministry on earth?*

1. Jesus knew what was expected of him by God (his "boss" if you will).
    a. He learned his Father's business **(Luke 2:46-47** and **2:49)**
    b. He was baptized, an indication of submission to God **(Matthew 3:13-17)**
    c. He often slipped away to pray (communicate with his boss) **(Luke 4:42** and **5:16)**
        - He prayed in private **(Matthew 14:23)**
        - He prayed before and during important events **(Matthew 14:22-36** and **9:28-30)**
        - He prayed in the garden and submitted to his Father's will **(Mark 14:32-36** and **Luke 22:39-46)**

2. Jesus knew his objectives, several of which were:
    a. To recruit and train his followers **(Mark 1:16-20)**
    b. To give us eternal life **(John 17:2)**
    c. To glorify the Father on earth **(John 17:4)**
    d. To bring us God's word **(John 17:14)**

3. Jesus knew his disciples (students) well.
    a. "I know my sheep and my sheep know me" **(John 10:14)**

   b. He prayed for his students **(John 17:9)**
   c. He knew heart motives and innermost thoughts **(Matthew 9:4, Matthew 12:25, Luke 5:22,** and **Luke 11:17)**

4. Jesus knew his subject—Scripture.
   a. He sat at the feet of experts **(Luke 2:46)**
   b. He often quoted and explained Scripture **(Matthew 4:1-11** and **Luke 7:27)**

5. Jesus "assessed" his disciples (students) throughout his ministry.
   a. He gave them tasks to accomplish **(Matthew 10:1-42)**
   b. He asked them questions **(Matthew 16:13-17)**
   c. He tested their faith **(John 11:1-44)**

6. Jesus used results to fine-tune his instruction.
   a. He clarified the disciples' thinking and purpose **(John 4:27-38)**

What other examples of Jesus' preparation can you find? In what ways do these examples correlate with your preparation for teaching?

Integrate

How does your preparation for teaching compare to the preparation Jesus did? Are you giving it your best?

QUESTIONS JESUS ASKED

"Jesus is The Answer"

Questioning has long been a favored strategy to encourage thinking and learning. Questions are also used as an indirect means of sharing information with students. Asking good questions requires skill and experience; it can be considered an art.

In creating a piece of art, one must know the subject very well, have a vision for the end product, determine the best approach to communicate the message, work carefully and creatively to convey the message, and adjust anything that does not contribute to the message. Likewise, when asking questions, one must know the subject, know the desired outcome, determine how to word the question to stimulate responses, and, based on those responses, make adjustments to obtain the desired results.

Investigate

One of the first things to investigate is the process of questioning in general. *Why do teachers (do you) ask questions of students? What do you hope to achieve by asking questions?*

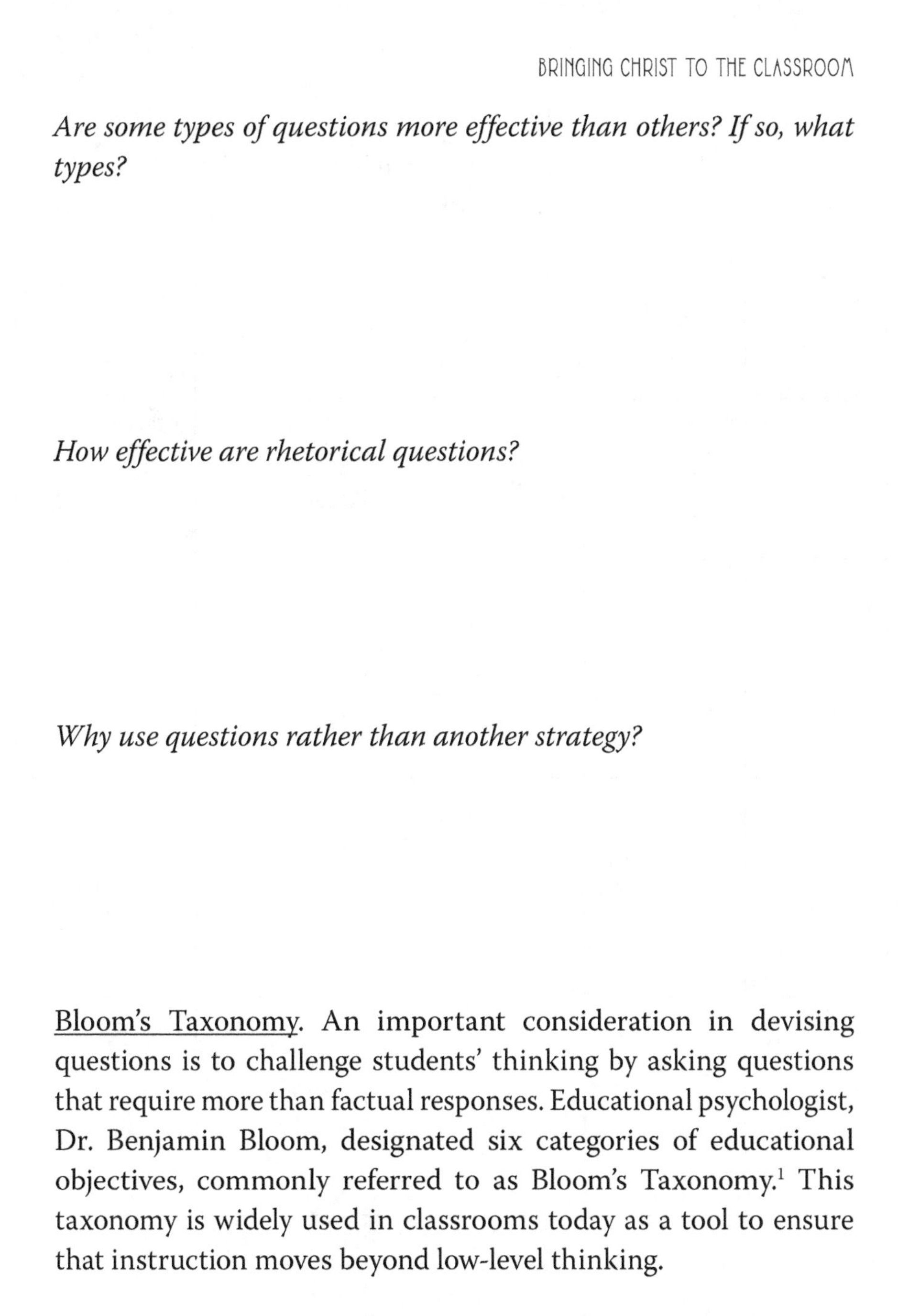

Are some types of questions more effective than others? If so, what types?

How effective are rhetorical questions?

Why use questions rather than another strategy?

Bloom's Taxonomy. An important consideration in devising questions is to challenge students' thinking by asking questions that require more than factual responses. Educational psychologist, Dr. Benjamin Bloom, designated six categories of educational objectives, commonly referred to as Bloom's Taxonomy.[1] This taxonomy is widely used in classrooms today as a tool to ensure that instruction moves beyond low-level thinking.

In extending this line of thought, *why did Jesus ask questions?* Dr. Roy B. Zuck, authoritative author of *Teaching as Jesus Taught* and senior professor at Dallas Theological Seminary, offers several points to consider. Use the chart[2] to record your findings.

Select one of the four gospels to analyze some of the questions Jesus asked. A red-letter edition of the Bible helps to isolate his words, making it easier to find his questions.

Scripture References	Jesus' Questions	Question Type; Bloom's Taxonomy Category	Purpose of Questions	Individual or Group Addressed and their Response
Matthew 5:13	"If the salt loses its saltiness, how can it be made salty again?"	Hypothetical question Bloom: Analysis level	Encourage reflection about what is means to be the salt of the earth.	Those listening to the Sermon on Mount No response noted

Illuminate

In the gospel book you just studied, approximately what percentage of Jesus' conversations and discussions consisted of questions? Based on your percentage, would you say questioning was a prominent technique used by Jesus?

Do you think the individuals or groups involved understood Jesus' questions? What types of questions and taxonomy categories did they understand? What types of questions and taxonomy categories did they not understand? You may want to add a column to your chart to record these responses.

Consider the purposes of Jesus' questions. *Was Jesus successful in accomplishing his purposes for asking questions? Why or why not?*

Think about the response Jesus may have wanted from each question. *Did the majority of the answers match Jesus' desired responses?*

Why do you think Jesus used questions as a teaching technique? Was it an effective strategy? Why? Why not?

Based on your findings, what questioning strategies did Jesus use? Compare your list with your current practices.

RESPONSES TO QUESTIONS

"Ever Be"

Not only did Jesus ask questions of others, they asked him questions to which he gave responses. Today those questions might be texted to him, perhaps thousands per day, but in Bible times questions were either asked in person or sent via a messenger. The responses Jesus gave to questions were memorable and often unexpected.

Responses to questions can be straightforward or involve a great deal of thought and consideration. Sometimes responses are given too quickly, without enough consideration, and the results may be detrimental.

Cultural Considerations. Cultural perspective makes a difference in how people respond to questions. Generally, European Americans are much more outspoken and respond quickly while looking the other person in the eye. In contrast, Native Americans, for example, are instructed to speak softly and not make eye contact out of respect. They are taught to think before they speak, indicating the worthiness of the question, and not say anything until they are certain their response is significant and accurate.[1] As the Bartlesville area has a sizable population of Native Americans, I have had the privilege of teaching many from a variety of tribes. Several Native American students have affirmed that these characteristics were part of their upbringing. One student confided the reason he does not make eye contact with others is because he believes the eyes are the gateway to the soul which, once seen, can be stolen. Having an understanding of that is just one example of the importance of learning the cultural perspectives of your students.

Nonverbal Considerations. It is easy to misinterpret nonverbal responses, especially if the responses are not given in person. Dr. Albert Mehrabian in his book, *Silent Messages,* asserts that 93% of communication is considered nonverbal making it more significant than verbal communication.[2] While some disagree with his research, the fact remains that much information can be gleaned from nonverbal cues (tone of voice, gestures, and facial expressions, etc.) that is missed when a conversation is not face-to-face. Because we did not witness Jesus' conversations, we cannot know the exact nonverbal context. Nevertheless, we can learn much about Jesus' responses to questions.

Investigate

One of the first things to investigate is the idea of "response" itself. *What motivates students to answer questions? Why do students not respond? What prohibits or limits their responses?*

What types of responses do your students typically give? Are their responses usually accurate? Are they carefully considered?

Continue the investigation by considering how Jesus used responses to stimulate his learners. Dr. Roy B. Zuck, authoritative author of *Teaching as Jesus Taught* and senior professor at Dallas Theological Seminary, offers several points to consider. Use the chart[3] to summarize and categorize the responses. You may want to add rows to the chart to analyze more questions.

Pick one of the four gospels in the New Testament and analyze Jesus' responses to some of the questions addressed to him. A red-letter edition of the Bible helps to isolate Jesus' words, making it easier to find his responses.

Scripture Reference	Person(s) Who Asked	Question(s) Asked	Situation(s) or Problem(s)	Jesus' Response(s)	Type of Response(s) by Jesus	Questioner's Response(s)
John **3:1-21**	Nicodemus	"How can a man be born when he is old?" "How can this be?"	Confusion Clarification	Jesus explained that he was speaking of spiritual rebirth and indicated how to be saved	Explanation, Questions, and More Explanation	No response is recorded at the end of their dialogue

Illuminate

Why do you think Jesus gave these types of responses? What types of thinking would be required to understand his responses?

Do you think the individuals or groups understood Jesus' responses? What examples confirm your ideas?

Were his responses effective in promoting change? Provide examples.

Integrate

Based on the types of responses Jesus used and how he used them, create a list of strategies that will promote change in your learners.

THE WEARY SHEPHERD

"O, Sweet Rest"

Bill and Jessie Elkins, a retired couple who had been missionaries to Guyana, attended our church when I was young. They said that one of the favorite hymns of those they served was "O, Sweet Rest" which tells of the rest heaven will provide. Years later when I was privileged to train teachers in Haiti, I saw first-hand what our missionary friends had described. To obtain daily food, Haitians toil from sunup to sundown, every day. They have no concept of "rest" on earth; therefore, they cherish the promise of a heavenly rest.

While the circumstances are different, educators do experience something similar in that the work never ends. It seems there is always someone who needs something. There are assignments to grade and reports to prepare, and, of course, there is always another meeting or planning session to attend. Educators rarely have a spare minute during the day. Lunch is a "gulp and go" moment. In the school setting, there is much truth to the adage, "There is no rest for the weary."

Investigate

Although paperwork was not on Jesus' "to do" list, Scripture indicates that he was often followed by crowds. It had to have been draining at times.

Read **Mark 6:6b-13** and **30-44**. After having been sent to preach about repentance, the disciples were trying to tell Jesus their experiences. People crowded around Jesus and the disciples to the point they could not eat so Jesus suggested they go someplace quiet to rest. However, the crowds followed them. "When Jesus landed and saw a large crowd, he had compassion on them, because they were like sheep without a shepherd. So, he began teaching them many things" **(Mark 6:34)**.

Despite a desire for privacy and rest, his weariness if you will, Jesus recognized the needs of the people and ministered to them. It was after this that he fed the 5,000, thus fulfilling both the spiritual and physical hungers of the people.

Describe the physical, emotional, and spiritual states of the disciples upon their return from ministry.

Speculate as to why Jesus had compassion on the crowd.

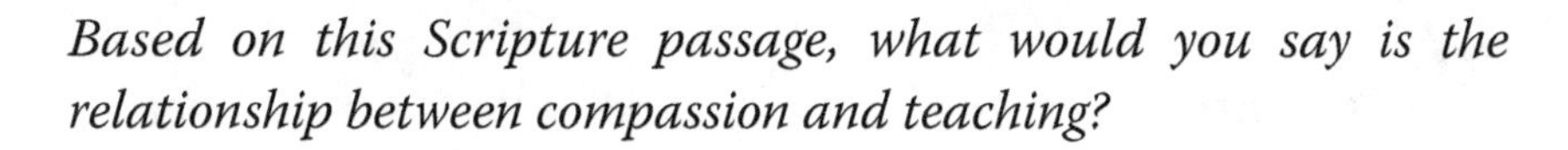

Based on this Scripture passage, what would you say is the relationship between compassion and teaching?

Illuminate

How do you react when it seems you are surrounded by students and colleagues, all wanting something from you?

What motivates you to overcome weariness and press on with the task?

What does the word "rest" mean to you? What kinds of things refresh and restore you?

Integrate

God has instructions for us as we serve him. Read **Matthew 11:28-30.** *How do you interpret "come to me" in times of weariness?*

Describe a time when Jesus provided the rest you needed.

What do you think Jesus meant when he said, "For my yoke is easy and my burden is light?"

What is the significance of being yoked together with Jesus in ministry to others?

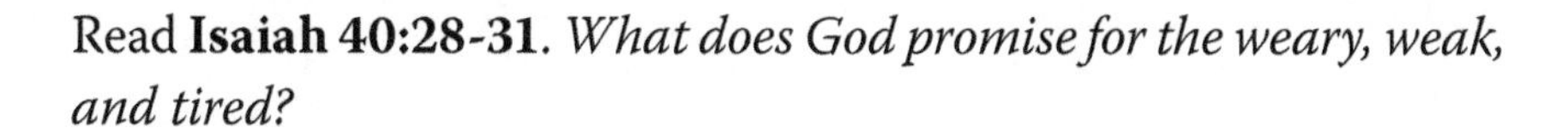

Read **Isaiah 40:28-31**. *What does God promise for the weary, weak, and tired?*

Describe a time when you waited for the Lord as instructed in the Isaiah passage. What was the outcome?

What steps can you take to soar like eagles and avoid burnout yet keep ministry as the central theme of your relationships with students and colleagues?

THE WOMAN AT THE WELL

"Fill My Cup Lord"
"Dip in to the Wells of Salvation"

Although much of the earth is covered by water, not all of the water is drinkable. In the United States, we take for granted that we can obtain clean water from our faucets. That is not the case in other places. In Haiti, for example, I observed people lining up at the only water spout in town to fill containers with trickles of water that, if consumed by Americans, would make us sick. Because water is crucial for survival, many organizations are working in countries around the globe to provide access to unpolluted water by digging wells, creating affordable filters, and teaching sanitation procedures.

Jesus used his need for water as a conversation starter **(John 4:1-42)**. After walking several hours, he was hot, tired, and thirsty so he asked a woman for a drink. Scholars help us understand several unusual things which occurred during this conversation.

<u>Travel Plans</u>. The first unusual fact is that Jesus went through Samaria to get from Judea to Galilee. At the time, there were two ways to travel north and south. The longer choice was to go through Gentile country, and the other choice was to go through Samaria. The relationship between Jews and Samaritans was so

hostile that many Jews preferred to go into Gentile territory rather than go through Samaria.

<u>Jews vs. Samaritans</u>. The second unusual fact is that Jesus talked to a Samaritan. Samaritans came into existence due to Jews marrying non-Jews, a direct violation of God's instructions **(Deuteronomy 7:3-4)**. Therefore, devoted Jews avoided Samaritans.

<u>Jewish Men vs. Women</u>. Third, Jesus talked to a female. Jewish men did not talk to women in public, not even to their wives.

<u>Background</u>. Fourth, Jesus talked to a woman with a questionable background. Scripture indicates she had five husbands and was not married to the man with whom she was living. While we do not know the reason for so many husbands, living with a man without marriage was definitely forbidden **(Mark 10:6-9)**.

<u>Trip to the Well</u>. Fifth, the time of day was unusual. Having grown up in the desert, I can tell you that a task like drawing water would have been done in the cooler parts of the day—morning or evening. The implication of her being there in the middle of the day is that she was avoiding others. Perhaps they taunted or ignored her. Perhaps she wanted to escape their stares and whispers. Whatever her reasons, she was making her trip for water, alone, in the heat of the day.

<u>Discussion</u>. Sixth, Jesus initiated the conversation. Jesus was hot, tired, and thirsty after his travels. He asked her for something he needed that she could provide. His question probably startled her and she in turn questioned him about his motives. He moved the conversation toward his ultimate purpose in talking with her by contrasting water from the well with living water. "Living" water was clean, dependably flowing, and bubbling up from a spring in the earth, cool and fresh. Well water was called dead or stagnant because it did not flow and was warm. To protect water in a well

from as much contamination as possible, it was usually covered, but that did not necessarily keep out dirt and critters. It was not clear, living water.

Given the choice of water from a well or from a spring, who would not want clean, cool water in the heat of the day? Jesus had her attention when he said he could provide something she desired. Her thoughts were on water she could drink that would temporarily satisfy her thirst. Jesus was talking to her about living water that would satisfy her soul eternally. By talking with her, he ignored religious and cultural restrictions to reveal God's love for her.

Investigate

Read **John 4:1-42**

Think about why Jesus "had to go through Samaria" **(John 4:4)**. *What was his purpose(s) or objective(s) in taking that route?*

What was Jesus' purpose (objective) for the woman? The disciples? The people from the town?

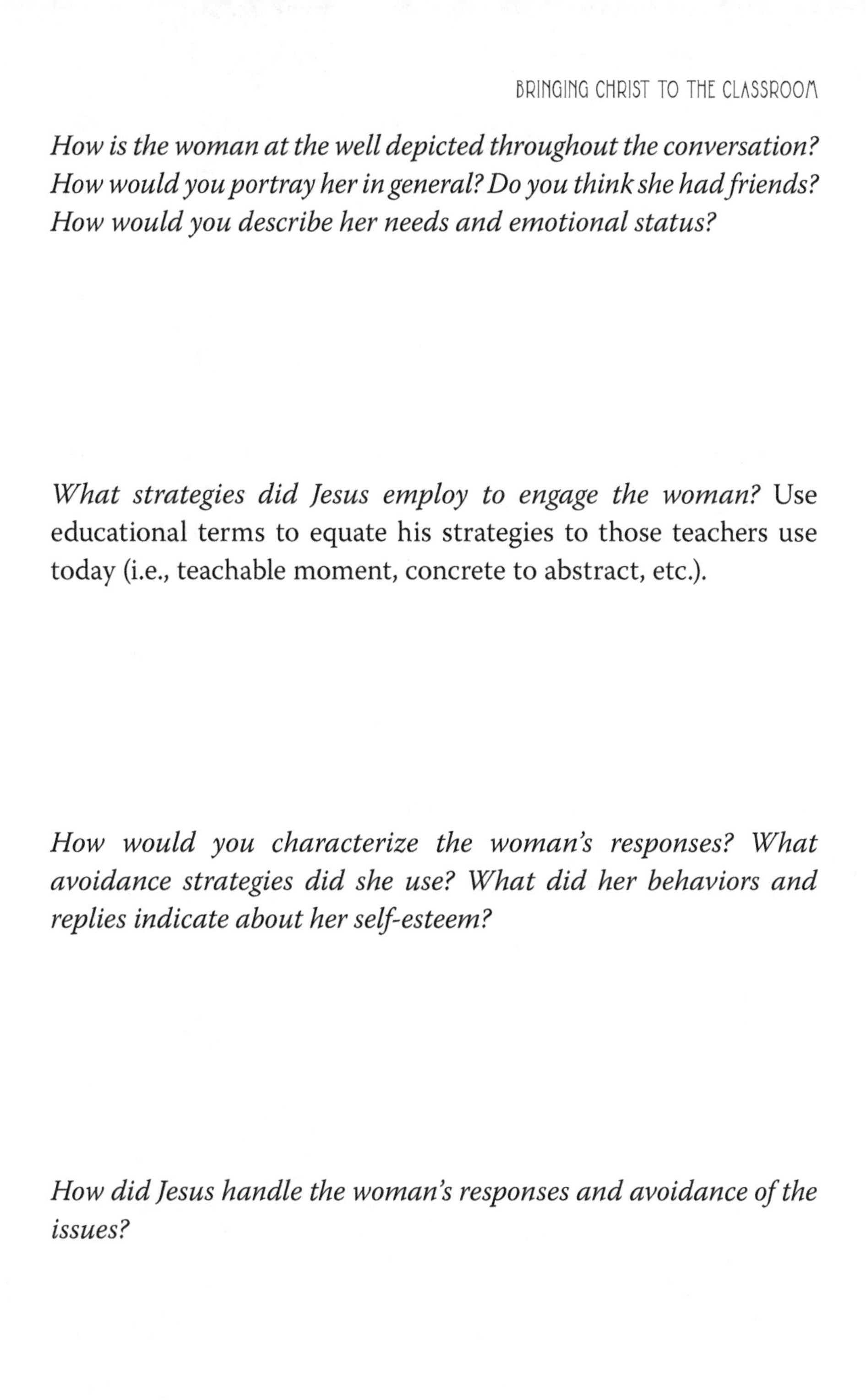

How is the woman at the well depicted throughout the conversation? How would you portray her in general? Do you think she had friends? How would you describe her needs and emotional status?

What strategies did Jesus employ to engage the woman? Use educational terms to equate his strategies to those teachers use today (i.e., teachable moment, concrete to abstract, etc.).

How would you characterize the woman's responses? What avoidance strategies did she use? What did her behaviors and replies indicate about her self-esteem?

How did Jesus handle the woman's responses and avoidance of the issues?

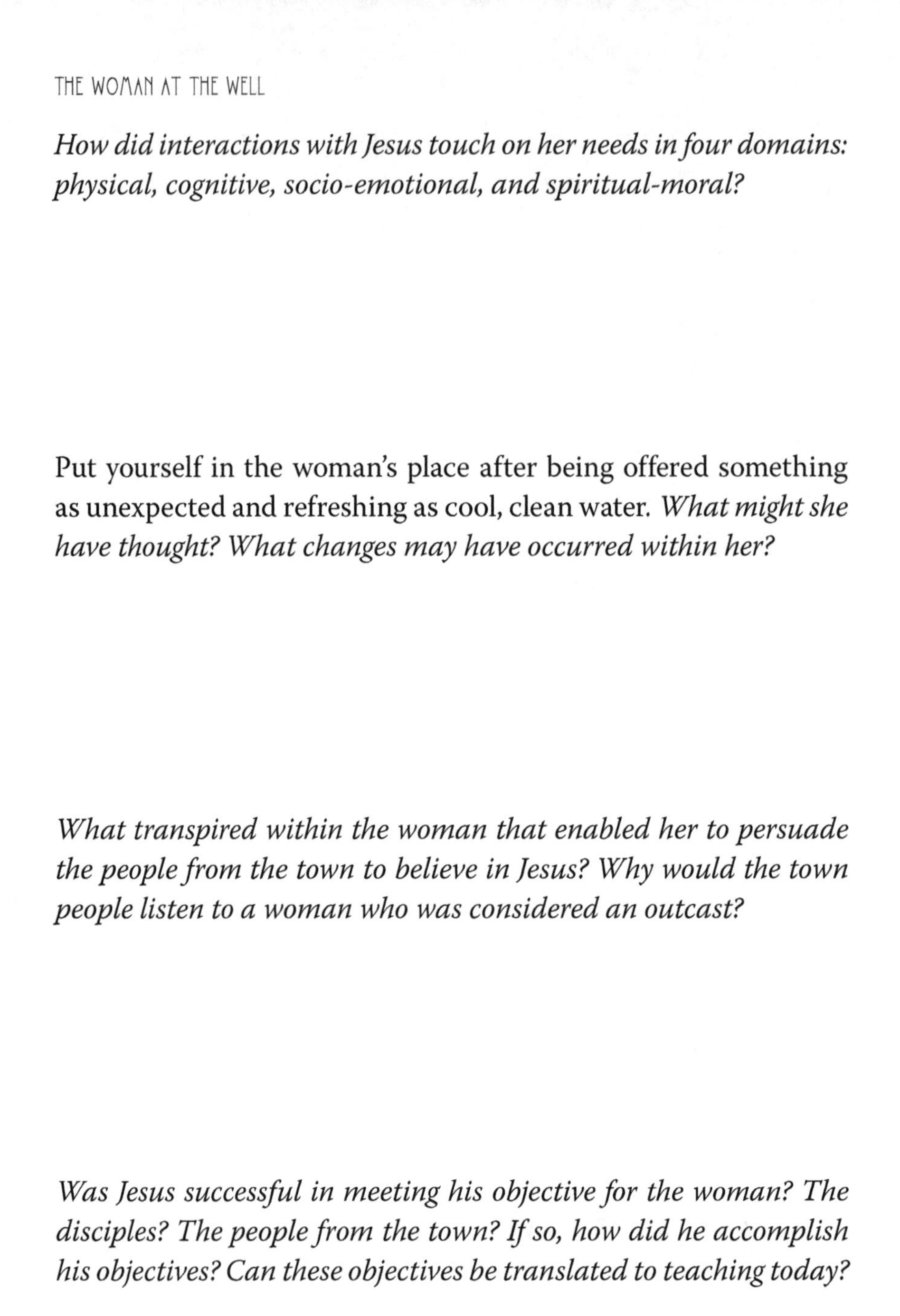

How did interactions with Jesus touch on her needs in four domains: physical, cognitive, socio-emotional, and spiritual-moral?

Put yourself in the woman's place after being offered something as unexpected and refreshing as cool, clean water. *What might she have thought? What changes may have occurred within her?*

What transpired within the woman that enabled her to persuade the people from the town to believe in Jesus? Why would the town people listen to a woman who was considered an outcast?

Was Jesus successful in meeting his objective for the woman? The disciples? The people from the town? If so, how did he accomplish his objectives? Can these objectives be translated to teaching today?

Illuminate

Although this is a bit of a stretch, imagine the woman at the well is the same age as your students and is assigned to your classroom. Based on the above descriptions of her:

What type of student do you think she would be?

What characteristics might she display in your classroom? How might she act before or after school, or during lunch, etc.?

What steps would you take to form a relationship with her?

What would be her greatest needs in the classroom? What would you do to help meet those needs?

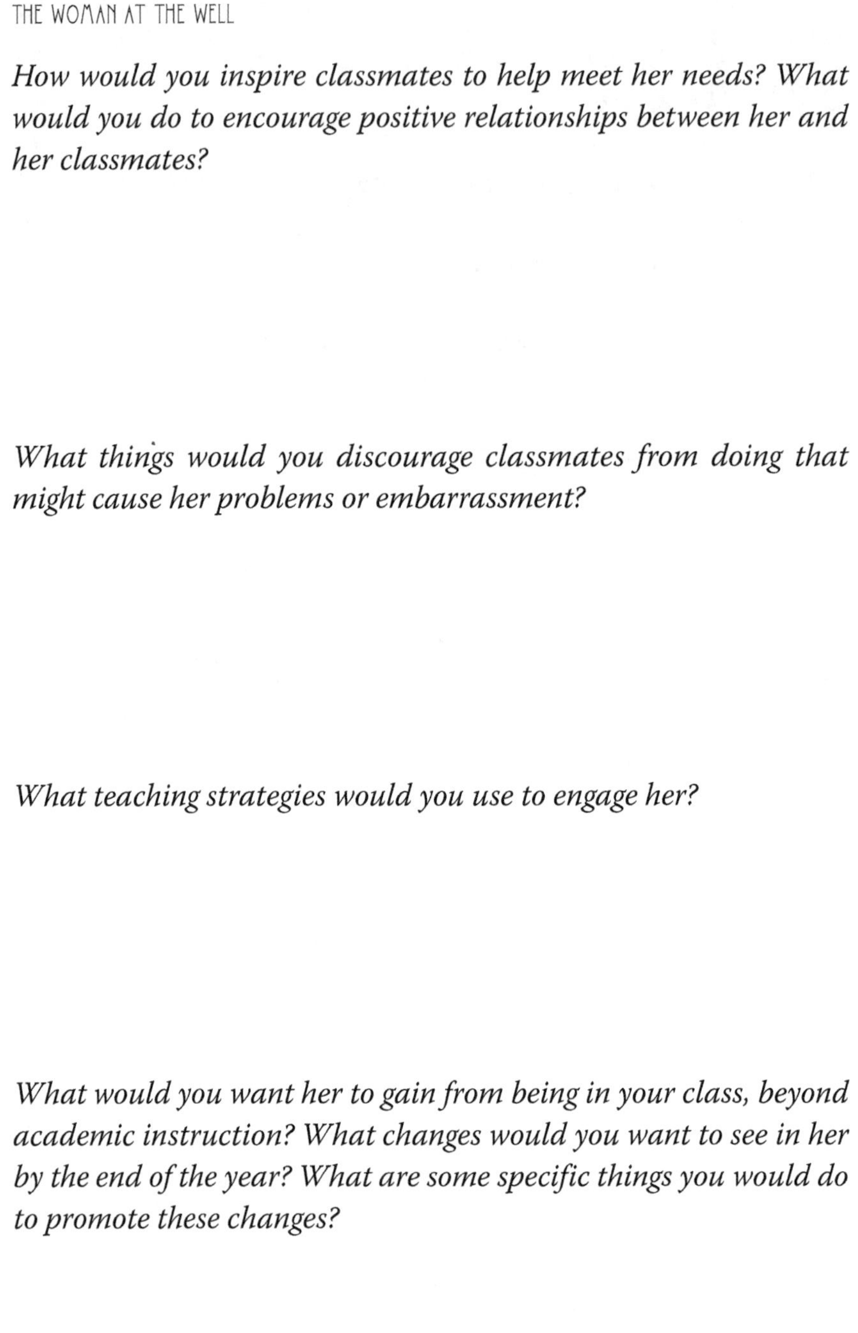

How would you inspire classmates to help meet her needs? What would you do to encourage positive relationships between her and her classmates?

What things would you discourage classmates from doing that might cause her problems or embarrassment?

What teaching strategies would you use to engage her?

What would you want her to gain from being in your class, beyond academic instruction? What changes would you want to see in her by the end of the year? What are some specific things you would do to promote these changes?

Core Needs. Author Dr. Kathy Koch, founder and president of Celebrate Kids, Inc., states that each person has five core needs that must be met "... in healthy ways so we can experience the hope and wholeness that God desires for us."[1] In hierarchal order, these are the core needs and the accompanying questions that must be answered:

1. Security: Who can I trust?
2. Identity: Who am I?
3. Belonging: Who wants me?
4. Purpose: Why am I alive?
5. Competence: What do I do well?[2]

How are Dr. Koch's core needs intertwined in the conversation between the woman and Jesus? Which of the woman's core needs did Jesus address? Did he fulfill the needs you previously stated? Did he fulfill the five core needs outlined by Dr. Koch?

In what ways did fulfillment of core needs change the woman's self-esteem?

Integrate

What teaching strategies used in this passage can you implement in your classroom?

How can you bring "living water" to your instruction?

In what ways can you develop hope, wholeness, and positive self-worth in your students?

Based on your findings, are there any adjustments to make in the way you view, relate to, interact with, or engage your students?

What additional insights from this passage can be integrated into your instruction and relationships with students and colleagues?

RELATIONSHIPS AND STUDENT ESSENTIALS

BALANCING TEACHING AND FRIENDSHIP

"What a Friend We Have in Jesus"
"Friendship with Jesus"

The advice for student teachers is to be friendly with their students but cultivate a professional relationship. Many studies conclude that the relationship with the teacher makes a significant difference in student motivation and achievement. The balance between building strong, friendly relationships and being too distant is like walking a tightrope, but Scripture indicates that Jesus succeeded in maintaining this balance. Other than the disciples, Mary, Martha, and Lazarus were probably the people with whom Jesus spent the most time. What can we learn about relationships between teacher and students from their interactions with Jesus?

Investigate

Respond to these questions as you read the passages: *What did Jesus want his friends and followers to learn from each of his encounters with Mary, Martha, and Lazarus? What were his objectives?*

- **Luke 10:38-42**–Mary as the student and Martha as the hostess/student

- **John 11:1-44**–Lazarus raised from the dead

- **John 12:1-11**–Mary anoints Jesus

Continue your investigation by answering a series of questions related to these encounters. *How did Jesus handle:*

1. *His duties as teacher vs. his friendship with Mary, Martha, and Lazarus?*

2. *Their request for help when Lazarus was sick?*

3. *Spending time with his friends? The disciples?*

4. *Compassion in the loss of a friend?*

5. *Interruptions?*

6. *Complaints and objections?*

7. *Gift-giving vs. lack of hospitality?*

8. *Something that was viewed as too lavish?*

9. *The teachable moment?*

10. *Going from the known to the unknown?*

11. *Priorities?*

12. *Personal loss versus: The needs of others? The task at hand?*

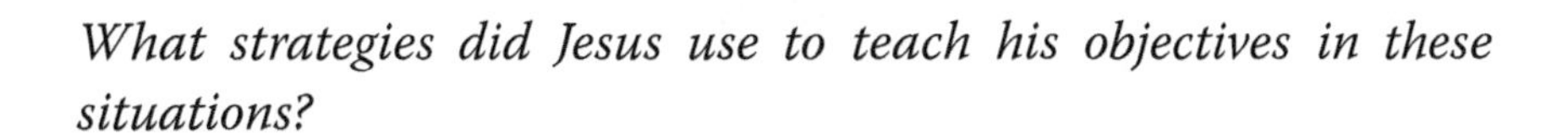

Illuminate

What strategies did Jesus use to teach his objectives in these situations?

How and what did Jesus adjust to meet the needs of these friends?

In what ways did Jesus follow the customs of the day? In what ways did he ignore them?

Did Jesus treat these friends any differently than his disciples and others?

Did these friends take advantage of their relationship with Jesus? If so, in what way(s)?

Were their expectations realistic?

How successful was Jesus in teaching these friends? The disciples? Others?

Did Jesus meet the objectives you listed above?

Integrate

Based on your discoveries about Jesus' friendship with Mary, Martha, and Lazarus, create a list of lessons to consider in balancing professional vs. personal relationships.

How can we apply those lessons to current and future relationships with students and colleagues?

BELONGING

"I Belong to the King"
"No, Never Alone"
"Now I Belong to Jesus"

Our family moved twice when I was a sophomore in high school. Although the first new school was smaller than our previous school, my Caucasian siblings and I were in the minority. It was difficult to go to a school where I did not know anyone and even harder when the majority of students were native Spanish speakers. Had it been permitted in our family, I would have stayed home with a stomach ache that started right before we left for school each day. In hindsight, I realize it was the lack of friends that brought on my symptoms. I did not belong.

You may have experienced this need to belong without realizing it. Imagine you register to attend a conference, are excited about the speaker, but wonder if you will know anyone. As you walk into the first session, you look around and see someone who motions you to sit in an empty chair. The discovery of a friend creates a sense of relief, comfort, and confidence as you realize you will not be alone. This is an example of a desire God instilled in us, the desire to belong.

Investigate

The concept of belonging appears as a theme in several children's stories you may remember including *The Velveteen Rabbit* whose search for belonging led him to wish he were real.[1] After a near-death experience, Snow White finds a place to belong with the seven dwarfs. Peter Pan and the Lost Boys found a place to belong in Neverland. The mother in *Love You Forever* declares her love for her son throughout his life by singing a song. He, in turn, sings the same song to her when she is old and then to his newborn daughter. [2] Their strong relationships fulfilled their need to belong. The fox in *The Little Prince* indicated he could not play with the prince because they had not established ties, but once they had, they would belong together.[3] Remember Mr. Rogers inviting you to be his neighbor? Millions of people today are asking others to be their "neighbor" via social networking. These are just a few examples of our desire to belong.

Many prominent authors include the concept of belonging in their works:

1. Dr. Abraham Maslow, psychologist and professor, features belonging in the middle of his Hierarchy of Needs.[4]

2. Erik Erikson, developmental psychologist and professor, proposed stages of psychosocial development. His Intimacy vs. Isolation stage centers on intimate relationships or belonging to each other.[5]

3. Dr. Josh McDowell, author and internationally-known speaker, describes three pillars that create the foundation for our true identity, the first of which is based on belonging.[6]

4. Author Dr. Kathy Koch, founder and president of Celebrate Kids, Inc., describes her model of core needs which includes belonging as the mid-point of the hierarchy.[7]

5. Dr. Chap Clark, author and professor at Fuller Seminary, talks about interdependence, or belonging, as being "in community with peers."[8]

These examples, along with numerous others, illustrate a manifestation of our desire to belong. Based on these few samples, we can imply that the desire to belong is a deep need.

Illuminate

Through Scripture, God discloses that he fulfills our need to belong. The promises God made to his people, Israel, in the Old Testament, can be applied to his followers today. Explore the verses and then record God's assurances that we belong to him.

- **Leviticus 26:12**

- **Deuteronomy 14:2**

- **Isaiah 43:4**

- **Isaiah 49:16**

In the New Testament, Jesus renews this commitment. Again, explore and then record assurances that we belong to Jesus.

- **Matthew 11:28**

- **Matthew 25:34**

- **John 15:19**

- **John 14:2-3**

- **Matthew 28:20b**

Paul continues the theme of belonging. As before, explore and then record these assurances.

- **Galatians 3:26, 29**

- **1 Corinthians 12:24b-25**

- **Hebrews 13:5**

Integrate

The idea of belonging as it relates to the classroom deserves more consideration than it would have in the past when most families fulfilled this need for their children.

How does belonging work in classrooms in general? How does it work in your classroom? How can you tell if a student belongs?

Compare characteristics of students whose need to belong is fulfilled with those who hunger to belong. How does belonging (or lack of belonging) affect behavior, motivation, participation, engagement, relationships, etc.? Prepare either a T-chart or Venn diagram to record your findings.

In what ways can you promote a sense of belonging in your students? How can they become more interdependent?

COMMUNITY

"The Family of God"

I love quilts. At quilt shows, a friend and I spend hours "oohing" and "aahing" at the handiwork of talented artists. Some of the most striking quilts, called crazy quilts, are mosaics of numerous pieces of material put together in a pattern dictated by the shape and size of the fabric. In some crazy quilts, the pieces of fabric may have been part of a shirt, dress, or tie that was deemed worthy of giving a second chance. Crazy quilts are typically embellished through the addition of elaborate embroidery, fragments of delicate lace, antique buttons, and fancy stitches. The patchwork of fabrics, the combination of colors, the meticulous stitching, and the embellishments are brought together in a deliberate design to create something beautiful. Due to all the variations, each quilt is unique, even if it uses the same pattern or fabrics as another quilt.

Investigate

Fashioning a quilt can be likened to creating community in the classroom. The instructor deliberately determines the pattern: the procedures and expectations necessary for the classroom to function smoothly. Students can be likened to the pieces of fabric, each unique in a variety of ways. Student backgrounds, experiences, personalities, and ways of learning correspond to the crazy quilt's embellishments. Quilters piece fabrics together and use embellishments to highlight various features of the quilt. In a similar manner, teachers begin the process of establishing the classroom environment at the beginning of a new school year by discovering students' unique characteristics and promoting a sense of unity. When everything comes together for the quilter, a new crazy quilt emerges. When everything comes together for the teacher, a new learning community is created. Teachers know that even with the same procedures, expectations, curriculum, and objectives, each classroom community functions in a distinctive manner due to the combination of students and their characteristics.

Read **1 Corinthians 12:12-31** and record your thoughts about the dynamics of community.

- Verses 12-13 – One body

- Verse 14 – One body with many members

- Verses 15-20 – Value of each

- Verses 21-24 – Interdependence

- Verses 25-26 – Equal concern: joys and sorrows

Illuminate

Building a classroom community is challenging for a variety of reasons. Some combinations of students are more challenging than others. Each instructor has his or her own ideas about how to bring together a group of students with all their distinctive characteristics to create a cohesive unit. One thing many educators implement within the first few days is learning as much as possible about each student. They intentionally seek to discover things about home life, educational background, strengths, weaknesses, interests, preferred ways of learning and engaging with material, etc. They use all of this information and more to begin forming relationships with students.

5 Love Languages. Some teachers also seek to discover the "love language" of each student. Best-selling author, pastor, and speaker, Dr. Gary Chapman, describes *The 5 Love Languages* and how they affect interactions.[1] Determining love language strengths will create a whole new level of connection with students. A free profile quiz is available at www.5LoveLanguages.com.

Discovering the uniqueness of each student is one of the first steps in building a classroom learning community. However, the idea of "community" is foreign to many students. *In what ways do you endeavor to create a community of learners? How do you blend your procedures, expectations, curriculum, and objectives with your current students to create a cohesive (quilted) classroom community?*

How do your procedures, expectations, etc., vary due to student characteristics? How do you determine what to allow, what to prohibit, what to overlook, or what to encourage?

Each instructor has his or her own ideas about how the classroom community should operate. There are those who say competition should be eliminated from the educational system. Instead, it should be collaborative. Others maintain that since the adult world is so competitive, students need to learn how to compete. *What do you think? What characteristics would be present in your ideal classroom?*

How does your classroom community operate? Consider some of the activities, assignments, and assessments in your instruction. Do their components align more with competition, cooperation, or collaboration?

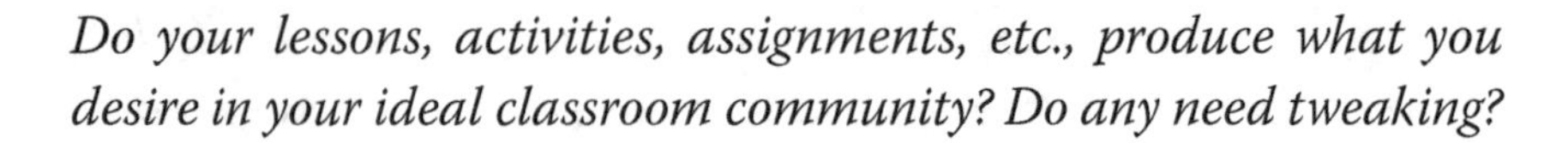

Do your lessons, activities, assignments, etc., produce what you desire in your ideal classroom community? Do any need tweaking?

How do you communicate the dynamics of "one body" to your students? How do you ensure that each student knows their value as a person as well as their value to the classroom community?

Read **Romans 12:3-8.** *Would your classroom community benefit from additional strategies to build a more interdependent unit? If so, what ideas do you have to accomplish this?*

Luggage vs. Baggage. Sharing in the joys and sorrows of others **(1 Corinthians 12:26)** is an integral characteristic of a cohesive classroom community. To promote this, a professor revealed that she begins each class with a time for students to communicate their burdens (personal concerns) and blessings (praises or celebrations), followed by a time of prayer. At the beginning of the semester, the professor introduces a metaphor they use during their sharing time. *Luggage* (their blessings) is excitedly packed for a vacation in anticipation of a change in schedule, a time of relaxation with family or friends, and an opportunity for renewal. On the other hand, *baggage* (their burdens) represents the negative "stuff" that originates from relationships, finances, stressful circumstances, etc. *Baggage* burdens us, drags us down, and limits our potential. To distinguish the types of their experiences, students indicate if they are bringing *baggage* or *luggage* with them to class that day. Their times of disclosure, followed by prayer, encourage collective compassion, develop trust, and create strong bonds of an interdependent community.

In a public-school setting, you cannot pray with your students out loud during class. However, *could you encourage students to share their luggage and baggage? Would this type of sharing contribute to building an interdependent community? If so, how might you implement it?*

COMPASSIONATE SHEPHERD

"Take the Name of Jesus with You"

Scripture offers several examples when Jesus focused on ministering to others in spite of weariness. Why did he pursue ministry rather than seeking rest? **Mark 6:34** states, "… he had compassion on them…. So, he began teaching them many things." Compassion appears to be the reason Jesus changed his plans to rest. Jesus could have easily shown them empathy (a sensitive understanding) or sympathy (a sorrowful expression), but that's where these feelings would have ended. Empathy and sympathy go just so far. Compassion, however, involves "a strong desire to alleviate suffering."[1]

Professor Patricia Jennings addresses this as she relates her classroom experience indicating that compassion provided the motivation for her to take action. "Sometimes when we feel empathy for another, our strong emotions can overwhelm our capacity to help."[2]

> … I noticed how the emotion [of sadness] impaired my ability to act in ways that might be helpful to these students. I realized that while my empathy for their situation was giving me a sense of how difficult their lives were, it wasn't motivating me to be helpful. Empathy involves experiencing the same emotion as the other person which can often be

> overwhelming. As I learned to manage my sadness, I was able to shift my empathy toward compassion—which involves the motive to help—and find ways I could be helpful.[3]

Investigate

Jesus did more than empathize or sympathize with people. He really knew them, their innermost thoughts, desires, and needs, and he had compassion on them. He took action by meeting their needs and promoting change in their lives.

Read the situation portrayed in **Mark 6:30-44** where Jesus took action by teaching the crowd and later by feeding them. His compassion for the people resulted in a change of his plans.

Read **Isaiah 52:7** and **Micah 6:8**. *What does the compassionate person do according to these passages? Create a list.*

Illuminate

How are these actions related to teaching? Add your responses to the list you created.

Integrate

What have your "beautiful feet" brought to your students? In your classroom or school, how have you or can you:

- *Bring good news?*

- *Proclaim peace?*

- *Bring good tidings?*

- *Proclaim salvation?*

- *Act justly?*

- *Love mercy?*

- *Walk humbly with your God?*

DIGNITY AND WORTH

"Not One Forgotten"

As I was considering taking education majors to our academy in Puerto Rico, I talked with an OKWU professor, a former missionary, who had extensive experience leading student trips to other countries. Dr. Mike Fullingim encouraged me to train students prior to trips to help prepare them for cultural differences and then de-brief with them afterward to process and amplify their experiences. Dr. Mike imparted a multitude of invaluable strategies and insights that prevented us from making novice mistakes or creating misunderstandings.

One concept Dr. Mike shared still resonates with me. My paraphrased version of the concept: when in another culture, we tend to compare our best with their worst. We do not make that comparison on purpose or even knowingly. As we are in the midst of those who have less, we observe their families, homes, shops, transportation, churches, etc. If we are not careful, we may unconsciously pity them or have a superior attitude toward them. Whether or not we are in another country or culture, we may make comparisons and subtly treat others with disrespect.

Respect is a foundation for relationships in any culture. When we respect someone, we acknowledge their value and significance. A respectful relationship transmits both dignity and worth to each person.

Investigate

Jesus interacted with many people who would have been considered insignificant or misunderstood by others. Because Jesus saw beneath the surface, accorded them dignity, and met their needs, their lives were radically changed.

Read the following passages. *How do you imagine the people felt before, during, and after their encounters with Jesus?*

1. **Mark 5:1-20**–Man possessed by evil spirits

2. **Mark 5:21-34**–Bleeding woman

3. **Luke 10:38-42** and **John 12:1-11**–Mary of Bethany

4. **John 8:1-11**–Woman caught in adultery

Illuminate

Consider: How did Jesus impart dignity and worth to those who were avoided, ignored, criticized, or rejected? What lessons can be learned from these interactions?

1. **Mark 5:1-20**–Man possessed by evil spirits
   He was an outcast living in a cemetery because nobody was able to control him, subdue him, listen to his continual wailing, or watch him bruise himself with stones. Then came Jesus. He met the man's need to be rid of the unclean spirits. Once the man was clothed and in his right mind, he begged to go with Jesus, an acknowledgement of the magnitude of change in his life. Jesus imparted dignity when he gave the man an achievable task. He instructed the man to tell his friends what God did for him. The man proclaimed what Jesus had done and everyone marveled.

2. **Mark 5:24-34**–Bleeding woman
   Jesus knew the woman had suffered for years. She had sought cures and doctors, spent all she had, and still grew worse. Her continuous bleeding made her untouchable **(Leviticus 15:25-33)** and anyone who touched her was unclean. Therefore, she lived in isolation. She may have thought of Jesus as her last hope and was willing to risk detection and denunciation. Although she was unclean and knew the risk, she touched Jesus and was instantly healed. Jesus immediately turned around to search for her in the midst of a great crowd, thereby establishing her worth. Her life changed when she reached out to touch Jesus. Scripture does not record if Jesus reached out to touch her. I like to think he did.

3. **Luke 10:38-42** and **John 12:1-11**–Mary of Bethany
The motives of Mary of Bethany appear to have been misunderstood by everyone. She was criticized more than once for her devotion to Jesus. Martha thought she was avoiding the work and complained to Jesus that Mary was not helping. Judas protested Mary's "waste" of an expensive ointment to anoint Jesus. In both situations, Jesus defended Mary by indicating her heart was in the right place. He also helped others look at Mary from a different perspective. In fact, **Mark 14:9** records that Jesus said her worshipful gesture would be widely imparted.

4. **John 8:1-11**–Woman caught in adultery
She was caught red-handed in an immoral act and hauled into the place of worship. There was no question that she was guilty of a crime for which the punishment was death. Everyone knew the severity of the consequences and were preparing themselves to carry out the sentence. Jesus took another approach to the situation. Instead of picking up stones as the others were ready to do, Jesus gave them a reading comprehension test. "How do these words apply in your life?" might be another way to interpret his question to the scribes and Pharisees. We do not know what Jesus wrote on the ground with his finger, but we do know that the religious leaders passed the comprehension test by not condemning the woman. Not only did Jesus save her life, he forgave her and provided the opportunity for her to make a new life for herself.

What other examples can you find of Jesus treating people with dignity and worth?

Integrate

Think of students (past or present) who have been misunderstood, avoided, ignored, criticized, or rejected by peers, family, or other adults. *What strategies did you use or could you use to impart dignity and worth to them?*

EMOTIONS

"Blessed Assurance"
"I Need Thee Every Hour"

Beginning in about 2005, I noticed the topic of "emotions" presenting itself quite often in educational journals and during classes. I likened the topic to a thread weaving itself in and out of our discussions throughout the semester. I soon added "emotions" as an official topic, and we now spend a class session considering how emotions affect the instructional environment by either helping or hindering learning.

Investigate

Scripture often refers to the heart when describing emotions. *How are emotions portrayed by the heart in these examples from the Old Testament?*

- **Genesis 6:6**

- **Genesis 42:28**

- **Deuteronomy 1:28**

- **Deuteronomy 15:10**

- **1 Samuel 2:1**

- **Psalm 13:2**

- **Psalm 33:21**

- **Psalm 143:4**

- **Proverbs 15:13**

Read the list of New Testament passages to determine how Jesus handled himself in a sampling of emotional situations. *What do you notice about how Jesus expressed emotions through his responses and reactions?*

- **John 11:32-36**–Jesus reacts to the death of Lazarus

- **Matthew 21:12-13**–Jesus clears the temple

- **Mark 6:31-34**–Jesus shows compassion

- **Matthew 23:37-39**–Jesus laments the rejection of his love and protection

- **Matthew 26:38**–Jesus in the Garden of Gethsemane

- **Mark 15:34**–Jesus on the cross

Illuminate

Influence of Emotions. Much is being written today about how emotions affect us. A sampling of ideas begins with *Emotional Intelligence,* by psychologist and award-winning author, Dr. Daniel Goleman, who describes emotional intelligence domains, beginning with becoming aware of our own emotions.[1] Author and expert on the brain, Dr. Eric Jensen, writes that at birth, six specific emotions are hardwired. However, even more emotions must be learned through instruction and modeling.[2] Author Rob Bocchino expands on that idea stating that emotional literacy consists of skills and understandings which can be taught and therefore can be learned.[3] Dr. John Gottman, professor and author, promotes emotion coaching in raising children.[4] Mindfulness, a growing emphasis in schools and culture, involves skills and strategies to filter and translate thoughts and emotions.

Emotions and the Brain. Brain science informs the conversation about emotions in that our personal experiences create emotions which in turn produce chemicals in our brain. These chemicals either aid the transmission of information in the brain (chemicals produced as a result of positive experiences) or inhibit information transmission (chemicals produced from negative experiences). In other words, the chemicals our emotions produce in our brains either help or hinder our capacity for learning.

Because emotions are so significant, we must be prepared to recognize when students are on emotional overload. We must realize they may not have learned appropriate emotional control at home and that we may need to teach them strategies to help regulate their reactions. By adding the ability to recognize and regulate emotions to the lengthy list of things already taught, educators give students a gift lasting a lifetime.

Integrate

Educators state that their students have more emotional baggage than ever before. Due to adverse situations, some students frequently have negative experiences and therefore continuously produce chemicals in their brains that hinder their capacity for learning. When they perceive situations as threatening or dangerous, they have hair-trigger responses. While others in the identical situation would not react in the same manner, within seconds these students are ready to protect themselves by fighting (aggressively defending themselves), fleeing (withdrawing), freezing (becoming motionless or rigid), or appeasing (giving up or submitting). God created our bodies to respond in these protective manners. Due to the chemicals flooding their brains, these students are prevented from doing well in the classroom. Learning is not their priority.

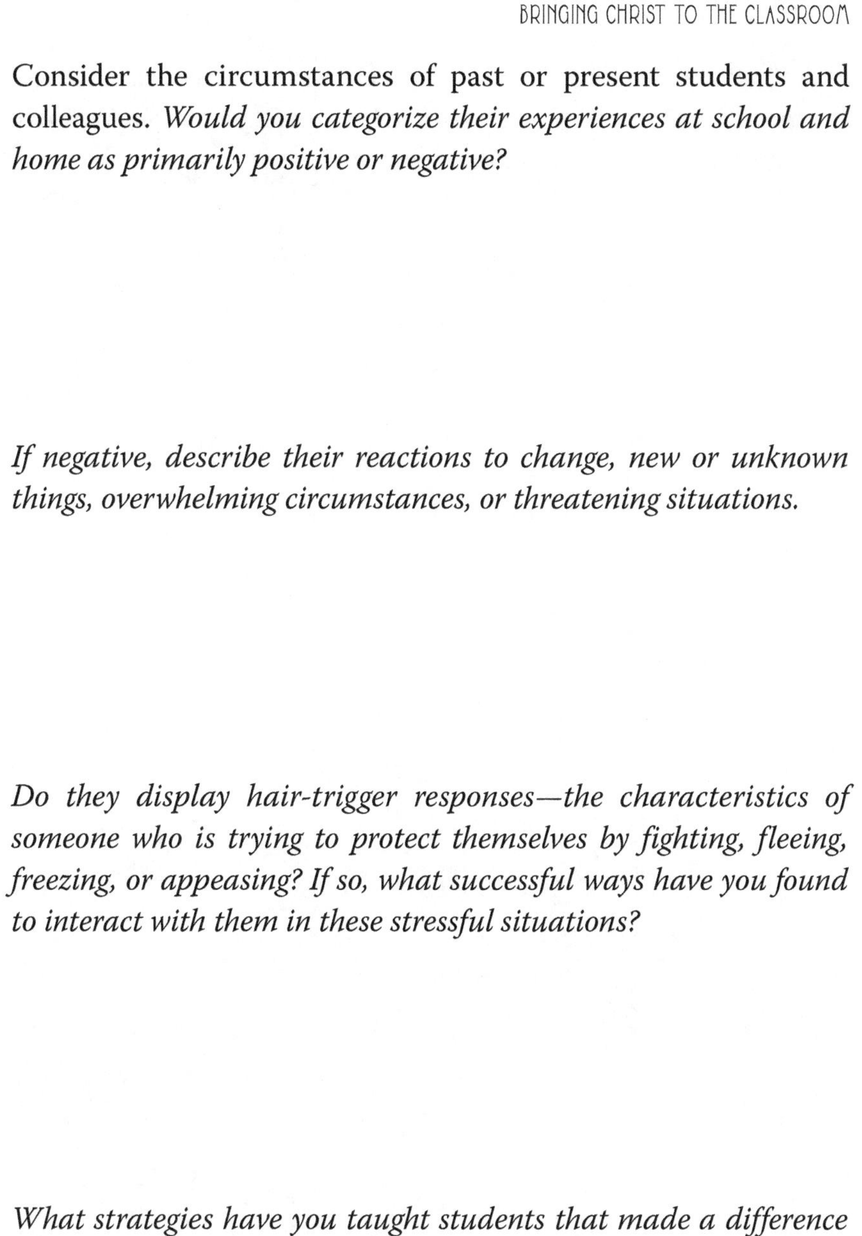

Consider the circumstances of past or present students and colleagues. *Would you categorize their experiences at school and home as primarily positive or negative?*

If negative, describe their reactions to change, new or unknown things, overwhelming circumstances, or threatening situations.

Do they display hair-trigger responses—the characteristics of someone who is trying to protect themselves by fighting, fleeing, freezing, or appeasing? If so, what successful ways have you found to interact with them in these stressful situations?

What strategies have you taught students that made a difference in their responses? Discuss your list with a colleague to learn what strategies he or she has successfully implemented.

What resources (school personnel, community agencies, reading materials, webinars, etc.) are available to assist you as you strive to understand how our emotions affect us?

ENCOURAGEMENT

"God Will Take Care of You"
"He Giveth More Grace"

How Full is Your Bucket? by Tom Rath and Donald Clifton describes an unseen bucket everyone has that is continually being replenished through positive interactions or drained by negative interactions.[1] Some people appear to have overflowing buckets as expressed by their consistent smiles and "can do" attitude. On the opposite extreme, other buckets appear to be empty. Through their ideas about our buckets, Rath and Clifton provide unique ways to think about our relationships with students, colleagues, family, and fellow believers.

Investigate

What part does encouragement play in relationships? A study of Barnabas will offer several things for us to consider. Our introduction to Barnabas comes in Acts where we learn he is a Levite from Cyprus who was given the name Barnabas (meaning son of encouragement) by the apostles **(Acts 4:36)**. The fact that they gave him this name indicates Barnabas had the gift of encouragement. The life of Barnabas is interwoven with Saul/Paul throughout the book of Acts.

In **Acts 9** we read of the life-changing encounter Saul had that transformed him from a persecutor of those belonging to the Way to a proclaimer of Jesus. It is understandable that the disciples in Jerusalem were afraid when Saul attempted to join them. However, Barnabas spoke on Saul's behalf and persuaded the apostles to accept him which freed Saul to preach boldly.

Read the passages chronicling the ministry of Barnabas. *Was encouragement involved? Make note of the relationship and interactions between Barnabas and Saul/Paul. How did their relationship progress?*

- **Acts 9:29-30**
  Saul is sent to Tarsus to escape those who wanted to kill him.

- **Acts 11:21-26**
  Barnabas looked for Saul and brought him to Antioch where they ministered together.

- **Acts 11:29-30**
  Barnabas and Saul carried relief money to elders in Judea.

- **Acts 12:25**
  John Mark (cousin to Barnabas) is with Barnabas and Saul.

- **Acts 13:1-4**
  Barnabas and Paul are "set apart" for ministry.

- **Acts 15:35-40**
  Disagreement over John Mark—Paul and Barnabas go their separate ways.

- **Colossians 4:10-11**
  John Mark is called a fellow worker and a comfort to Paul.

- **Galatians 2:1**
  Paul and Barnabas go to Jerusalem (reconciled).

- **II Timothy 4:11**
  Paul requests John Mark be brought to him as he was valuable to him in ministry.

Illuminate

While we do need to be careful in reading between the lines in the Bible, what can we learn from the life and ministry of Barnabas? *What roles did Barnabas play in the ministry of Saul/Paul? What roles did Barnabas play in the life of his cousin, John Mark?*

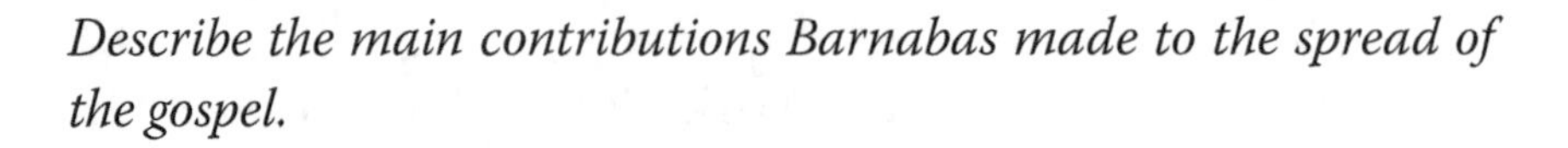

Describe the main contributions Barnabas made to the spread of the gospel.

In what ways did Barnabas "fill the buckets" of those around him? What part did encouragement have in his relationships?

We know the division over John Mark resulted in more churches being reached in a shorter amount of time because splitting up provided two teams to minister in different locations. However, disputes like this can easily shut down relationships. *Put yourself in the place of Barnabas and Paul. How do you think they got over this depletion of their buckets so they could effectively minister and eventually reconcile with each other? How do you think John Mark transitioned from being rejected by Paul to being a comfort and useful fellow worker?*

An interesting fact to consider is that in the first Scripture references Barnabas is listed before Saul. We might think of Barnabas as a mentor to Saul. Eventually there is a shift, and Paul's name is listed first. We know that Paul was significantly more prominent than Barnabas in the end. *What might be the implications of this change in listing their names?*

What is the "job" of a mentor? Does the mentor/student relationship always last a lifetime?

Integrate

Do you consider yourself an encourager? What would your students say about you as an encourager? How often do you find yourself filling the buckets of others? Do you need to improve? If so, what are some specific ways you can be more encouraging?

Would others say you deplete their buckets? If so, how can you make amends? What steps can you take to prevent this from happening in the future?

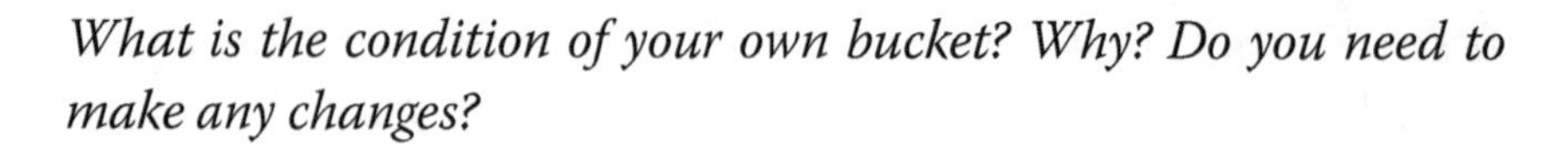

What is the condition of your own bucket? Why? Do you need to make any changes?

Describe someone who was your mentor. How did that person encourage you? What did that person teach you? How are you passing along these lessons?

Is there someone you could encourage? Someone you could mentor? If so, what action will you take?

FEED MY LAMBS

"Safe in the Arms of Jesus"

"Feed my lambs," Jesus instructs Peter in an exchange during which Peter confirms his love for Jesus **(John 21:15-17)**. The second time Jesus asks about Peter's love for him, Jesus tells him to "tend my sheep." A third time Jesus questions Peter's love and directs him to "feed my sheep." What is the significance of this conversation between Jesus and Peter? What was Jesus trying to communicate? If Jesus speaks about caring for sheep three times, it must be noteworthy for Christian educators to consider.

In analyzing this conversation, the emphasis is typically on the form of the word "love" for which Jesus uses "agape" meaning a perfect love, yet Peter responds with "phileo" meaning more of a friendship love. By using "agape," Jesus asks Peter to examine the depth of his commitment. In addition to the significance of Peter's love, Adam Clarke and Ralph Earle indicate there is another change in word usage when Jesus refers to sheep as both *"bosko"* meaning "to feed" **(John 21:15** and **17)** and *"poimaino"* meaning "take care of, guide, govern, defend" **(John 21:16)**.[1]

In this passage, Jesus communicates his instructions for those who, like Peter, are leaders. Educators can extend the metaphor to the classroom with the teacher as the shepherd and students as sheep, but *what does it mean "to feed, take care of, guide, govern, and defend" sheep? What is expected of "shepherds" of the classroom?* List several ideas here before continuing.

Investigate

A Shepherd Looks at Psalm 23 by Phillip Keller describes shepherds as "... gentle, kind, intelligent, brave and selfless in their devotion to their flock."[2] He continues by saying that for shepherds, "... there is no greater reward, no deeper satisfaction than that of seeing his sheep contented, well fed, safe and flourishing under his care.... From early dawn until late at night this utterly selfless shepherd is alert to the welfare of his flock."[3]

Read **John 10:1-16**. *Create a list of insights into characteristics and responsibilities of the shepherd.*

When describing sheep lying down in green pastures in **Psalm 23:2** (referring to their sense of safety, security, and contentment), Keller informs us that "it is almost impossible for them [sheep] to be made to lie down unless four requirements are met...." For sheep to feel safe enough to lie down, the sheep must be

1. Free of all fear
2. Free from friction with others of their kind
3. Free of ... pests [flies or parasites]
4. Free from hunger[4]

How does the shepherd in **John 10:1-16** *provide freedom, security, contentment, and nourishment?*

How do the characteristics of a shepherd as outlined thus far relate to those of an educator?

Illuminate

Which of the shepherd's characteristics do you find in yourself? Which are lacking? Compared with Keller's comments about the shepherd's reward, how does teaching bring satisfaction?

What does it mean to lay down your life for the good of your students? What does it mean for a teacher to be selfless?

How well do you know your students, beyond knowing their names? Are you the kind of leader students will follow? Are you worthy of their trust?

What is the "pasture" for students? What provisions can you make for their safety, security, and pasture?

What kinds of things threaten students?

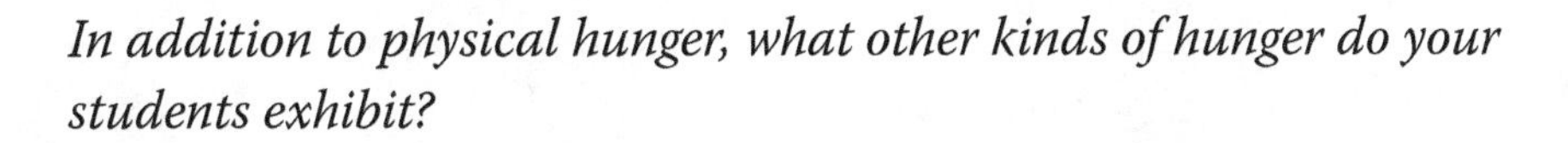

In addition to physical hunger, what other kinds of hunger do your students exhibit?

What can you do to free your students from fear, friction with others, pests, and hunger?

What signs indicate that your students are flourishing?

Integrate

List ways you are serving and will serve your students by "feeding, taking care of, guiding, governing, and defending" those in your charge.

IDENTITY

"I'm a Child of the King"

Many find it difficult to establish their identity and determine what to do with their lives, yet identity (or lack thereof) significantly affects how we go through life. Identity extends inward into our hopes, dreams, and desires. It also extends outward to our ways of relating to others and the variety of situations that occur in our lives. Identity includes what we believe about ourselves, our sense of purpose in life, and our world view. We typically think of teenagers as the ones searching for their identity, but for some, the search lasts into adulthood.

How do we as humans establish our identity? Our earliest notion of who we are typically comes from our immediate family. Lasting impressions about our identity are formed by how they treat us as well as what they say to us and about us. In establishing identity, the sphere of influence widens as we get older, from our family to those in our environment—family friends, teachers, peers, neighbors, and others. We are also affected by our experiences, activities, and how we spend our time.

Investigate

What does Scripture say about Jesus' identity? Throughout the Old Testament we learn about his coming to earth and gain glimpses of his identity. Several examples of the foretelling of Jesus' life and identity are found in **Isaiah**. *Make note of what these passages indicate about the identity of Jesus.*

- **Isaiah 7:14**–Emmanuel (God with us)

- **Isaiah 9:2-7**–Unto us a child is born

- **Isaiah 11:1-5**–Righteous Judge

- **Isaiah 28:16**–Precious Cornerstone

The New Testament records the fulfillment of Old Testament prophecy about Jesus' life on earth and grants us the opportunity to learn more directly about his identity. An examination of the book of **Luke** reveals numerous ways Jesus' identity was communicated. *When reading passages in this partial list, consider what was being conveyed about Jesus' identity.*

- **Luke 2:46-49**–Jesus found in the Temple

- **Luke 3:21-22**–Beloved Son

- **Luke 4:16-21**–Jesus reading in the Synagogue

- **Luke 4:31-34; 4:40-41**–Demon declarations

- **Luke 9:7-9**–Herod asks who Jesus is

- **Luke 9:18-21**–Jesus asks about others' perceptions

- **Luke 9:28-36**–My Son

Obviously, there is no question about Jesus' identity. As God's Son and one of the Trinity, Jesus' identity is matchless. Scripture records that he knew who he was, he knew his purpose, and he communicated his identity from a young age. For a more in-depth study, search for additional passages about Jesus' identity in Matthew, Mark, and/or John.

What does Scripture say about our identity as Christians, made possible through Christ? Upon what do we base our identity? *Read this partial list of passages indicating God's view of us and how much he loves each and every person.*

- **Genesis 1:26-27**–Created in the image of God

- **Isaiah 43:21**–Our purpose

- **Romans 3:22-24**–Justified, Forgiven

- **Romans 6:3-4**–New life
- **Romans 8:1-2**–Set free
- **Romans 8:37**–Beloved conquerors
- **1 Corinthians 12:27; 12:12-26**–Body of Christ
- **2 Corinthians 5:17**–New creation
- **Galatians 2:20**–No longer I, but Christ
- **Galatians 3:26-4:7**–Heirs
- **Ephesians 2:1-10**–God's workmanship
- **Ephesians 3:14-19**–Christ's dwelling
- **Ephesians 1:4-5**–Chosen, Adopted
- **Ephesians 4:22**–New creation

- **Colossians 3:1-4**–Raised with Christ

- **Colossians 3:12-17**–God's chosen ones, holy and beloved

- **I John 3:1**–God's children

- **Revelation 2:17**–A new identity given by God

- **Revelation 22:17**–Bride of Christ

Develop a statement to summarize God's view of you. Why did God create you? What is your identity in Christ? How does your identity in Christ enable you to minister to your students?

Illuminate

Some students are so caught up in their negative circumstances that they believe their life will not improve. Their natural tendency is to compare themselves with others and feel inferior. When working with children like this, my social worker friends assist them with strategies to help them cope with their situations. One of the things they tell these children is that "normal" is only found as a setting on the washing machine. They encourage these children not to make comparisons. They want them to understand that everyone has a different "normal" due to their unique circumstances in life.

Consider how your identity was shaped during childhood, positively or negatively, by each of the listed groups and experiences. If working with others, share your experiences.

- Family

- Family friends

- Teachers, Coaches, Pastors, and other important adults

- Peers

- Education

- Cultural background

- Experiences, Travel

- Activities, Hobbies

- Use of Time

Quest for Identity. It is commonly believed that teens build on their childhood ideas about identity by deepening and expanding their knowledge and experiences. Some become passionately interested in pursuing a specific line of study or occupation which may (or may not) be soon replaced by another. Author and professor Erik Erikson describes this adolescent search for identity as a type of time out during which teens experiment with different roles to determine their identity.[1] This viewpoint implies that we form our identity through the interaction between nature and nurture, a common perspective among scholars who consider identity formation as an extrinsic search process.

Author and professor Dr. Chap Clark presents a contrasting viewpoint. "... the quest for our identity ... is located in our ability to get a complete picture of God's handiwork as he created it."[2] Dr. Clark proposes that finding our identity is an *intrinsic discovery process* through which we

> ". . . discover the person buried beneath the performance.... The Scriptures make it clear that who we are is decided before we are even born.... The childhood and adolescent journey ... is to get past any and all messages that would stand in the way of appropriating this truth in the depth of [our] souls."[3]

Johari Window. Yet another perspective on identity is discovered through consideration of the Johari Window, by psychologist and professor Dr. Joseph Luft, which is a unique tool used to study interpersonal relationships as they connect to behavior, feelings, and motivation. The Johari Window is divided into four windowpanes or quadrants, each designated as an aspect of our self-knowledge as well as others' knowledge and perceptions of us. As you read descriptions of the quadrants, visualize a window divided into four windowpanes or sections:

1. The *open* windowpane consists of behavior, feelings, and motivation we know about ourselves and others know about us.
2. The *blind* windowpane involves behavior, feelings, and motivations that others see in us, but we do not know about ourselves.
3. The *hidden* windowpane contains behavior, feelings, and motivations we know but others do not.
4. The *unknown* windowpane represents behavior, feelings, and motivations not known by others or ourselves.[4]

For example, a person with a large *open* quadrant is open to the world which "...implies a developed and ever-growing state, an experiencing, doing, enjoying, struggling, changing, creating, dreaming, agonizing, renewing, problem-solving, appreciating state of being with self and with others."[5] A person who does not "...share personal reactions and feelings, especially about *what is going on at the moment,*" may be perceived as psychologically distant[6] and has a large *hidden* quadrant.

As Christians, we realize that only God accurately sees the entire "window" of each person. However, we can learn a great deal about ourselves by using the Johari Window in two ways: (1) prayerfully considering each windowpane as it relates to ourselves and our relationships, and (2) discussing our conclusions with intimate friends and seeking their input.

Examine the four window quadrants to consider additional ways to analyze your relationships. It may be helpful to create a list of life dimensions (intellectual, emotional, spiritual, social, physical, professional, etc.) and consider strengths and weaknesses in each area as well as ways you may improve in your weak areas. Discussion with a trusted friend might be beneficial.

What insights do you discover about yourself (your identity) from examination via the Johari Window?

View of Self. Sociologist and professor Charles H. Cooley wrote about the social self with a concept that has come to be called "The Looking-Glass Self." The illustration is that of individuals reacting to the image in the looking glass or mirror. Based on what we see in the mirror, we imagine how we appear to other people and what they think of us. This provides us with a perception of ourselves which can be positive or negative.[7]

Foster Cline, M.D. and Jim Fay, founders of the Love and Logic Institute, put it this way: ". . . I don't become what you *think* I can, and I don't become what I think I can. I become what I think you think I can."[8] In other words, we get our ideas about ourselves from what we think others think about us.

Take a minute to reflect on that last statement—we get our ideas about ourselves from what we think others think about us. *Do you have a personal example of this? Have you been swayed by what you think others think of you? What evidence of this do you see in your students?*

Integrate

Identity Transformation. In *See Yourself as God Sees You,* Dr. Josh McDowell, author and internationally known speaker, offers three ways to transform an identity. *How can his ideas be adapted to students in your classroom?*

1. "A transformational environment includes people who will model the truth about who they are in Christ."[9] *How can you model your identity in Christ to your students?*

2. "A transformational environment is one in which the truth about your identity is clearly taught from Scriptures."[9] *How can you transmit Scriptural truths about identity to your students?*

3. "A transformational environments provides a context of loving, intimate relationships."[9] *Does the context of your classroom environment promote loving relationships?*

Consider one or two students as you respond to the next questions.

- *How have their experiences formed their sense of who they are?*

- *Have these experiences influenced them in positive ways? Negative ways?*

- *Analyze your students' interpersonal relationships by using the perspective of the Johari Window. Do they have "open" personalities? Do they "hide" things about themselves? Are they "blind" to their strengths and weaknesses? Are there ways you can help them discover the persons they are becoming or have the potential to become?*

- *Based on the concept that we get our ideas about ourselves from others, what ideas are you transmitting to these students? What else could you do intentionally to instill positive ideas within these students?*

Use this information to reflect on how you could assist students in their understanding of themselves as "fearfully and wonderfully" created by God ***(Psalm 139:14)****. How could you help them realize they are "… unique, unrepeatable miracles of God"*[10] *and, prayerfully, eventually discover their purpose in life—their identity in God's eyes?*

INTERACTING WITH "ONE ANOTHER"

"We Are One in the Spirit"

The learning process is greatly affected by interactions between teachers and several groups of people: students, parents, other teachers, building specialists, support staff, and administrators. The quality of relationships within one of these groups spills over into relationships within the remaining groups. Getting along with others is a crucial life skill.

Investigate

What does Scripture have to say about our relationships with others and in the context of community? *Study the "one another" passages of the New Testament and describe your observations about interacting with others.* (Note: Some versions of the Bible do not use the phrase "one another" for all of these passages; therefore, you may need to check other versions if you desire to find that specific wording.)

- **John 13:34-35**–love

- **Romans 12:10**–be devoted to; honor others above self
- **Romans 12:16**–live in harmony
- **Romans 15:5**–be likeminded toward
- **Romans 15:7**–accept
- **1 Corinthians 12:25**–care for
- **Galatians 5:13**–serve
- **Galatians 6:2**–bear burdens
- **Ephesians 4:32**–be kind; forgiving
- **Colossians 3:16**–teach; admonish
- **1 Thessalonians 4:18**–comfort

- **1 Thessalonians 5:11**–encourage; build up

- **Hebrews 3:13**–encourage

- **James 5:16**–confess faults to; pray for

- **1 Peter 4:9**–offer hospitality

- **1 Peter 5:5**–submit to; clothe with humility toward

Illuminate

Create a list of concepts you derive from the "one another" passages. *What do these passages say about relationships? Community? Interdependence?*

How do the concepts on your list translate to your relationships with students, parents, other teachers, building specialists, support staff, and administrators?

Integrate

Based on your findings, what actions will you take to integrate these "one another" concepts into your interactions and relationships with people in your life at school? What adjustments and changes will you make to enhance your interactions and relationships?

How will you integrate these "one another" concepts into your instruction, learning activities, environment, etc.? What will you create or eliminate in your classroom? What will you encourage or discourage?

MODELING EFFECT

"Tis So Sweet to Walk with Jesus"

Sixteen-year-old Glenn sat in his seat during the invitation at the end of a youth convention service while his younger brother, Jim, went forward to accept the call to ministry as a vocation. Upon return, Jim noticed that Glenn was upset. When pressed, Glenn said, "I know I am called to be a junior high teacher and coach, but I guess that doesn't count." As Glenn did, we tend to consider a call from God in relation to pastoring a church or going to another country. We do not think of other types of occupations as ministry.

Whether we acknowledge it or not, our lives are reflections of our beliefs transmitted through our interactions with others. We model our values as we go about our daily tasks and, therefore, we are constantly ministering to others. Even though not legally permitted to invite students to seek God in a public school setting, all educators serve enormous mission fields. Throughout their careers, educators can powerfully impact more lives through daily contact with students than most pastors do in a lifetime of preaching.

Modeling, imitating those around them, is the primary way young children learn. Parents are often surprised upon the realization that their child's negative behavior is an imitation of their own conduct. While it may not be as prominent later in life, the modeling effect still plays a role in each of our lives. We pay attention to and are affected by the character, conversation, and conduct of others.

Investigate

What kind of impact does an educator have through their character, conversation, and conduct? At the end of his 26th year as a middle school science teacher and basketball coach, Glenn suddenly died at age 48. As the shock waves spread, numerous current and former students, faculty, and staff came to his family's house to express their condolences and share how he had affected their lives through his influence as their teacher, coach, or co-worker. The retired superintendent of his school district revealed that he met Glenn at the back-to-school all-district teacher rally Glenn's first year when Glenn stood up, stated he thought they should begin every meeting with prayer, and then sat down. The superintendent said he agreed and, because of Glenn, they began every meeting with prayer for the remainder of that superintendent's tenure. In addition to this revelation, person after person shared how Glenn sought them out when they were floundering in middle school, talked to them about their behavior or attitude, and changed the direction of their lives. Many indicated Glenn inspired them to become teachers, coaches, pastors, or missionaries. He had modeled his relationship with God and his love for others through his character, conversations, and conduct.

Think about your day-to-day instruction and interactions with students. As an educator, you probably spend more time during the school year with your students than do their parents. You, in turn, may spend more time with your students than you do with anyone else in your life during that same time period. *Due to frequent interactions with you, what have students learned about your character from your conversations and conduct? Do they see a difference in you compared to other teachers? Do they look at you as a positive role model?*

Illuminate

Jesus affirmed that he imitated his Father **(John 5:19)** and portrayed God's great love for us **(John 3:16)**. By coming to earth, Jesus became the supreme role model for his disciples and for us. Daily interactions with Jesus enabled his disciples to learn about his divine character through his conversations and conduct, and their lives were dramatically changed. Even small things that Jesus did had a lasting influence as portrayed by an example which occurred after his death and resurrection.

Read **Luke 24:13-35**. They did not recognize Jesus until he took the bread, gave thanks, broke it, and gave it to them. While it can easily be argued that God opened their eyes, I like to think it had something to do with seeing Jesus do something very familiar. Because praying and breaking bread were things he had done (modeled) multiple times in their presence, their familiarity with Jesus caused something to click and they realized who he was. They had absorbed his essence and recognized his actions from having spent so much time with him. When Jesus spoke, people listened and learned. They knew him through his character, conversation, and conduct.

Integrate

Countless educators can report of former students who thanked them for doing or saying something, usually something small, that made a difference. It is rewarding to watch a student mature and succeed in life, even more so if the student comes back to express their gratitude. It is humbling and fulfilling to be the recipient of such a tribute. *Describe a similar experience you or a colleague have had.*

We used to ask each other if there would be enough evidence to convict us if we were on trial for being Christians. *Despite not being able to proclaim that Jesus is the way to heaven, do your students know, from what you model, that you love, serve, and imitate God* **(Ephesians 5:1-2)**? *Would they have enough evidence to come to this conclusion through your character, conversation, and conduct? How does your life count for Christ?*

Glenn's life as an educator did count and his influence as a role model spread far and wide due to his passion for God and for teaching. His life counted as he made a difference in the lives of his family, friends, students, and co-workers. He made a difference in my life too—he was my brother.

PRESSURE TO CONFORM

"Hold to God's Unchanging Hand"
"Near to the Heart of God"

The pressure to conform is a powerful influence which can be positive or negative. Educators witness this phenomenon in many ways as students strive to fit in with their peers. At a certain age, many students want to wear clothing of the same design, style their hair in a similar way, have matching backpacks, or listen to the "in" music. They are willing to conform to gain and keep friends. A multitude of concepts such as a sense of identity are involved in the decision of whether or not to conform to the expectations of others.

Why do humans conform? Some would say we are motivated by peers, position, popularity, power, pleasures, prestige, and prosperity, all of which are temporal concerns that can drive human behavior.

What do we relinquish when we conform to the negative? Some would say we abandon our character, communication, conduct, convictions, customs, and attitudes.

Why and how do we overcome the negative pressure to conform? Some would say the deciding factors include our personal convictions, our sense of identity and belonging, our personality characteristics, our past experiences and training, and our knowledge of the situation.

Standing up to peers and doing the right thing are not always easy and not always popular. The right choice is often a difficult one which could lead to being misunderstood, abandoned, criticized, or worse.

Investigate

Jesus was repeatedly challenged by those who thought he was not adhering to religious and cultural expectations. Read the passages and respond to the three sets of questions for each situation to determine how Jesus handled this pressure to conform to what others believed he should do and be. You may want to create a chart to organize your responses.

1. *What was the dilemma? What issues were involved?*
2. *What were the religious and cultural expectations? What were others trying to accomplish?*
3. *What enabled Jesus (and Joseph) to overcome the pressure to conform? What strategies did Jesus use to conquer the pressures put on him by others?*

- **Matthew 4:1-11**–Jesus' temptation

- **Matthew 9:9-12**–Dinner with the tax collector

- **Matthew 12:1-13**–Pharisees and Sabbath laws

- **Matthew 15:21-28**–Canaanite woman

- **Matthew 26:47-54**–Garden of Gethsemane

- **John 3:1-17** & **19:38-42**–Nicodemus asks questions

- **Matthew 1:18-25**–Joseph's decision about Mary's pregnancy

Illuminate

Think about Daniel and his friends, in a foreign land, standing firm on their belief in God which led to the blazing furnace and the lions' den **(Daniel 1-6).** The psalmist, a captive in Babylon, gives us an indication of some of the emotions they may have felt:

> By the rivers of Babylon, we sat and wept when we remembered Zion. There on the poplars we hung our harps, for there our captors asked us for songs, our tormentors demanded songs of joy; they said, 'Sing us one of the songs of Zion!' How can we sing the songs of the LORD while in a foreign land? **(Psalm 137:1-4)**.

It would be challenging to resist conforming to the expectations of others in circumstances like these. There is a kind of mourning that occurs when placed in difficult situations. You know what is right, but it is hard to go against others. Perhaps you are the only one who is opposed. In this situation, you have to decide if you will stand alone or go along with everyone else. It is as though you are in a strange land. How can you be true to yourself, your beliefs, and your God? "How can we [you] sing the songs of the LORD while in a foreign land" **(Psalm 137:4)**?

What strategies did Daniel and his friends use to avoid compromising their beliefs ***(Daniel 1-6)****?*

How did they "sing the songs of the Lord?"

What situations in your students' lives compel them to conform, whether it is to positive or negative peer pressure?

Integrate

From your lists of strategies used by Jesus and Daniel and friends, which might help conquer the pressure to conform to the negative influences in your life?

What kinds of things could you implement that would promote positive motivators and minimize negative pressures in your classroom and school?

What assistance can you give to students, parents, or colleagues who are trying to do the right thing but appear to be by themselves in a foreign land?

RESILIENCY

"It is Well with My Soul"

There is often a fine line between success and failure. When faced with failure, some retreat or give up. They do not learn from their experiences and may end up repeating the same mistakes in the future. Those who are resilient learn from their errors and use failure as motivation to improve and grow.

Resiliency has to do with our response to the difficult circumstances of life. How easily do we cope with and adapt to adversity? Resilience depends on a variety of factors such as support from family and friends, a sense of belonging and autonomy, and problem-solving skills as well as personality traits like a positive outlook, persistence, self-confidence, courage, and hope. A resilient person looks for life lessons from all situations, whether positive or negative.

Investigate

The life of Peter presents an interesting study of someone who was eager to learn, had good intentions, often failed or did not get it, but still persisted and became a leader among the disciples as well as within the church in Jerusalem. Interestingly, Peter is often first in the list of disciples, and we know more about him from Scripture than many of the other disciples.

Read the passages to determine how Jesus used various events in Peter's life to sculpt him into the one he called the Rock. *What characteristics are revealed? Are they positive or negative?*

Jesus calls Peter

- **John 1:40-42**
- **Matthew 4:18-20**
- **Luke 5:1-11**

Peter walks on water

- **Matthew 14:22-33**

Peter declares Jesus is Messiah

- **Matthew 16:13-28**

Peter offers to build shelters at the Transfiguration

- **Matthew 17:1-13**
- **Mark 9:2-13**
- **Luke 9:28-36**

Jesus washes the disciples' feet

- **John 13:1-17**

Jesus predicts Peter's denial; prays that Peter's faith will not fail

- **Matthew 26:31-35**
- **Mark 14:27-31**
- **Luke 22:31-38**
- **John 13:36-38**

"Watch and pray" in the Garden of Gethsemane

- **Matthew 26:36-46**
- **Mark 14:32-52**

"Put your sword away" in the Garden of Gethsemane

- **Matthew 26:50-54**
- **John 18:10-11**

Peter disowns Jesus

- **Matthew 26:69-75**
- **Mark 14:66-72**
- **Luke 22:54-71**
- **John 18:15-18**
- **John 18:25-27**

Peter runs to the tomb and believes

- **Luke 24:12**
- **John 20:1-10**

Jesus reinstates Peter

- **John 21:15-19**

Peter addresses the crowd at Pentecost

- **Acts 2:14-41**

For an even deeper study into the lessons Peter learned from Jesus, read "the rest of the story" in Peter's own words in the books of **1st and 2nd Peter**. *What resilient characteristics are revealed?*

Based on your study of the previous passages, in what ways was Peter a failure? In what ways was Peter resilient? How did each situation shape his life?

In what ways did Jesus interact with Peter to ultimately produce the Rock?

How would you describe a student who is resilient? What characteristics does a resilient student display in an overwhelming situation or when faced with failure (or potential failure)?

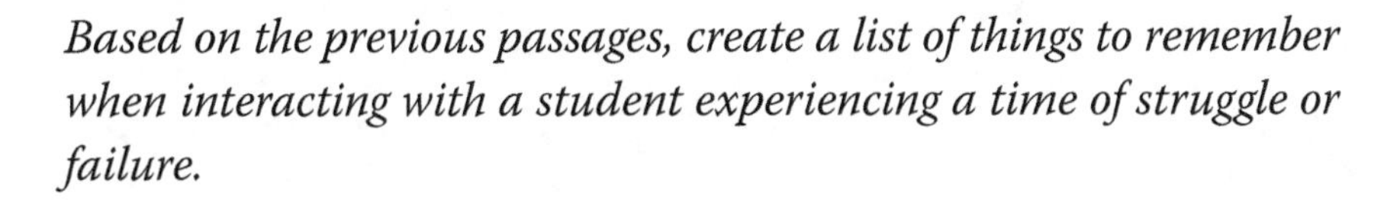

Based on the previous passages, create a list of things to remember when interacting with a student experiencing a time of struggle or failure.

Record strategies you could use with students to either encourage or instill resilience.

SAFE HAVEN

"Safely Sheltered"

Psalm 107:30

"They were glad when it grew calm, and he guided them to their desired haven."

Betty Ludlow, an artist who came to Christ due to the door-to-door evangelism efforts of my Dad, painted two images for our church in Phoenix. The painting for children's church was an interpretation of the angel watching over a boy and girl crossing a treacherous bridge. As a young child, I remember being comforted by the idea of God sending angels to help us.

The second painting, placed behind the pulpit in the front of our small sanctuary, was a striking image of Jesus with open arms. The Scripture reference below the artist's signature was **Matthew 11:28** which says, "Come to me, all you who are weary and burdened, and I will give you rest." The painting which portrayed his kind eyes, full of compassion, and his arms, outstretched in invitation, cemented in my mind the fact that I could run into those arms whenever I needed consolation. Both paintings were transported into our new church building, but due to the moveable partition behind the pulpit, the painting of Jesus was hung on a side wall in the sanctuary. What we had not realized until then was that Jesus' eyes looked directly at you no matter where you were in the room.

It was if he were always watching over you out of love and concern, no matter where you might be.

The concepts of watching over students, comforting them, inviting them with open arms, consoling them, loving them, and being concerned about them describe some of the characteristics of the classroom as a safe haven. The safe haven classroom is a place where students know they are welcomed and wanted. In a safe haven, someone is watching out for their best interests and listening to them. A safe haven is a place where they can depend on those around them. It is a place where they are respected and can contribute. It is a place that imparts a sense of peace and hope.

Investigate

The story is told of orphaned European children who, after World War 2, lived in refugee camps and could not sleep because they were afraid they would be homeless and hungry when they awoke. Someone suggested putting them to bed with a piece of bread. The children were then able to sleep peacefully with the assurance they had food for tomorrow.[1] Once the reality of stability and protection sank in, they found a "safe haven" and replaced their fear worry with trust.

Someone said that "fear not" is the most frequently-used phrase in the Bible. It makes sense. As adults, we are afraid of many things. We are fearful of the fate of the economy, government policies, safety in our homes, potential weather disasters, and rising prices for food, utilities, insurance, etc. Fear, accompanied by worry, can easily keep us awake at night. Many children face fearful, threatening situations daily. School is often the only place they feel some degree of calmness, protection, and safety. They need that safe haven; in fact, they crave it.

1 John 4:18 indicates that "... perfect love drives out fear...." *What examples of this have you experienced in your students? How do you lessen students' fears and worries?*

Jesus exhibited a "safe haven" environment showing children the respect they deserve when he scolded the disciples for turning them away **(Mark 10:13-16)**. It was unusual for a rabbi to recognize children in this manner because children were not considered as significant as adults. The disciples perceived children as unworthy of Jesus' time. Not only did Jesus take time to talk to the children, he held them, laid hands on them, and blessed them. Then, Jesus elevated their status by indicating the Kingdom of God belongs to children!

What can educators do to create a safe haven environment? How can we communicate that each day is a new beginning? How can we instill biblical concepts like love, peace, hope, and joy in our classrooms?

Illuminate

Invitational Education. An approach to education that mirrors Jesus' attitude toward children, Invitational Education, uses the metaphor of "teaching as inviting" and promotes the idea that students are to be treated with respect as valued contributors with untapped potential. Among other things, they describe "inviting" or "disinviting" comments, behaviors, signage, and environmental factors that send subtle (or not-so-subtle) messages, positive or negative. For example, is it respectful to keep checking the time or reading text messages when talking to students rather than using eye contact and actively listening? What nonverbal message do these kinds of conduct send to students? Negative comments, situations, and environments can create an overall "disinviting" impression on everyone.[2]

In what ways are your classroom and school "inviting" or "disinviting" to students?

The "We" of the Classroom. Establishing a warm, inviting atmosphere and treating each student with respect and dignity are ways to begin creating a safe haven. Over and over in educational research, the relationship between the teacher and the student is identified as the most important ingredient in determining student success. Several authors have written about the invisible "*we*" of the classroom, citing statements teachers make such as, "Today *we* are going to...." or "*We* need to...." as examples of its existence. Using the word "*we*" indicates a dependency on each other—*we* work cooperatively to accomplish the task.

Do you refer to "we" in the classroom? If so, how? Does it contribute to an overall feeling of connectedness?

Classroom Motif. Educators know that not everything goes well in the classroom and that students do undesirable things. Reactions in these situations make a difference in relationships with students and in the classroom atmosphere. Many educators would agree with the Scriptural "creation-fall-redemption-restoration motif"[3] as a basis for interactions and classroom structure. *What would you add to the initial lists provided?*

Creation–"In the beginning God created the heavens and the earth" **(Genesis 1:1)**.

- In the classroom, educators "create" an environment by what they expect, what they permit, what they prohibit, and what they promote.

Fall–Eve and then Adam disobeyed God **(Genesis 3:6-7a)**. They fell from grace.

- Students are going to blow it, disobey, make mistakes, and disappoint us. In other words, they will fall from grace.
- Educators understand these "falls" are typically due to the students' circumstances and characteristics.

Redemption–God loves us so much that he sent Jesus to take pay the consequences for our sin **(John 3:16; Ephesians 1:7)**. Therefore, we are redeemed because God forgives us. We can begin to build a strong personal relationship with God. We can also pass along this forgiveness and redemption to others.

- Educators understand that God has a purpose in placing students in their classrooms.
- Educators love students enough to hold them accountable for their actions.
- Educators forgive students which "redeems" them.

Restoration–God restores us to commune with him **(1 John 1:9; Zephaniah 3:14-17; Hebrews 8:12)**. He remembers that we are human **(Psalm 103:6-18)** but does not remember our sin **(Isaiah 43:25)**.

- Educators take an interest in students and make efforts to develop professional relationships with them.
- Educators accept students as they are, created in God's image **(Genesis 1:27)**.
- Educators "restore" students by making it clear that each day is a fresh start, an opportunity to join in the learning experiences.
- Educators welcome students as participants in the classroom community.

Restorative Practices. Ideas which may help implement the "creation-fall-redemption-restoration" motif come from a movement in education called Restorative Practices.

> ... to be 'restorative' means to believe that decisions are best made and conflicts are best resolved by those most directly involved in them. The restorative practices movement seeks to develop good relationships and restore a sense of community in an increasingly disconnected world.[4]

"'Restorative' means changing your own attitude, and it also means believing in students even when—and especially when—they seem to be behaving badly."[5] A restorative practices continuum provides a framework for educators to "... build a relationship based on students' new image of you as someone who cares and has feelings, rather than a distant authority figure."[6]

Restorative Practices' Social Discipline Window illustrates four combinations of two factors involved in discipline: (1) control (setting limits and discipline) and (2) support (nurture and encouragement). High support and high control are identified as a

> ... 'restorative' response to wrongdoing.... This is when those in authority exercise their control, refusing to accept inappropriate behavior, but do so in a caring and supportive way.... By engaging with young people, we can hold them accountable in an active way. Then we are doing things WITH them. But when we simply hand out punishments, we are doing things TO them. Or when we take care of their problems and make no demands, we are doing things FOR them. And when we ignore their behavior, we are NOT doing anything.[7]

Integrate

In working with student teachers over the years, I passed along several things for them to consider in their classrooms:

- We cannot control what happens. The two things we can control are: (1) our reactions and (2) our attitudes.
- Build respectful relationships with students and colleagues.
- Treat each day as an opportunity for a fresh start.
- Connect positively with each student daily, no matter how brief the connection.
- Be firm, fair, and consistent.
- Say nothing to a student in content, tone, or body language that you would not say to an adult.
- Avoid sarcasm. (One student teacher called it "scarcasm" due to the harm caused to his students by sarcastic words.)
- Have high expectations for everyone and provide support as needed.
- Hold students accountable.

- Do not take misbehavior personally. It is not about you.
- Be careful what you "threaten" to do. If you threaten it, you must follow through.
- Arguing with students does not work.
- Actively listen, non-judgmentally.
- Give students choices as often as possible and accept what they choose.
- Ask for student input.
- Ask how you can assist individual students.
- Admit your mistakes, apologize, and make restitution as appropriate. Learn from your errors!
- Patience, perseverance, and prayer are priorities!

Do you agree with this list of advice for student teachers? What would you add to it? What would you take away from it?

An interesting exercise is to create a T-chart, dividing **Isaiah 43:21-27** into small segments. Determine God's perspective in the first column to generate a "school" perspective in the second column.

Can the teacher in you relate to how God itemizes Israel's many transgressions listed on your chart? Do you have difficulties blotting out student transgressions? How do you handle students who "fall

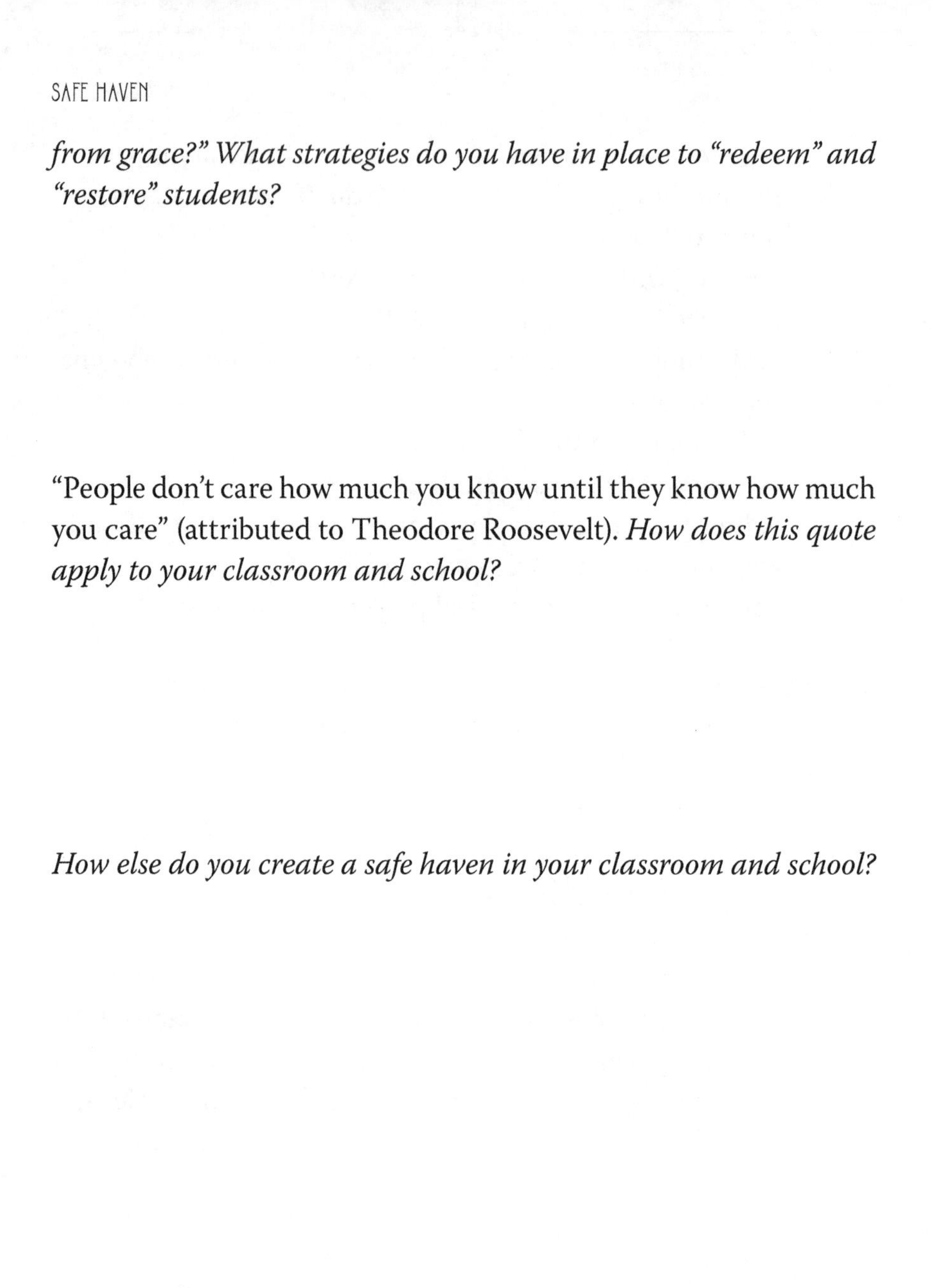

from grace?" What strategies do you have in place to "redeem" and "restore" students?

"People don't care how much you know until they know how much you care" (attributed to Theodore Roosevelt). *How does this quote apply to your classroom and school?*

How else do you create a safe haven in your classroom and school?

THE SEARCHING SHEPHERD

"Love Found Me"
"The 90 and 9"
"Seeking for Me"

Experienced educators can tell you about students who stray for one reason or another. Among the minor examples would be stories about students who daydream more than they study or those who would rather be outside. Educators often spend a great deal of time trying to keep students like these on task. **Isaiah 53:6a** tells us about straying sheep: "We all, like sheep, have gone astray, each of us has turned to our own way;...." *Describe instances of students who have "turned to their own way" and gone astray.*

Investigate

Read **Ezekiel 34:11-16**. *What do you notice about the description of how God will search for his sheep (Israel)?*

Jesus extends the discussion of searching for wandering sheep. Read **Matthew 18:12-13** and **Luke 15:3-6**. Note that the shepherd cared about *all* the sheep, even the one who strayed away, and throws a party when the lost sheep is found.

Describe characteristics of the searching shepherd. What does the shepherd do for the sheep?

Describe characteristics of the sheep. How do they need the shepherd?

Illuminate

Read **Luke 15:11-24**. Although typically titled "The Lost Son," some would say it should be titled "The Searching Father." *Compare the characteristics of the searching shepherd with those of the father. How are the shepherd and the father similar? How are they different?*

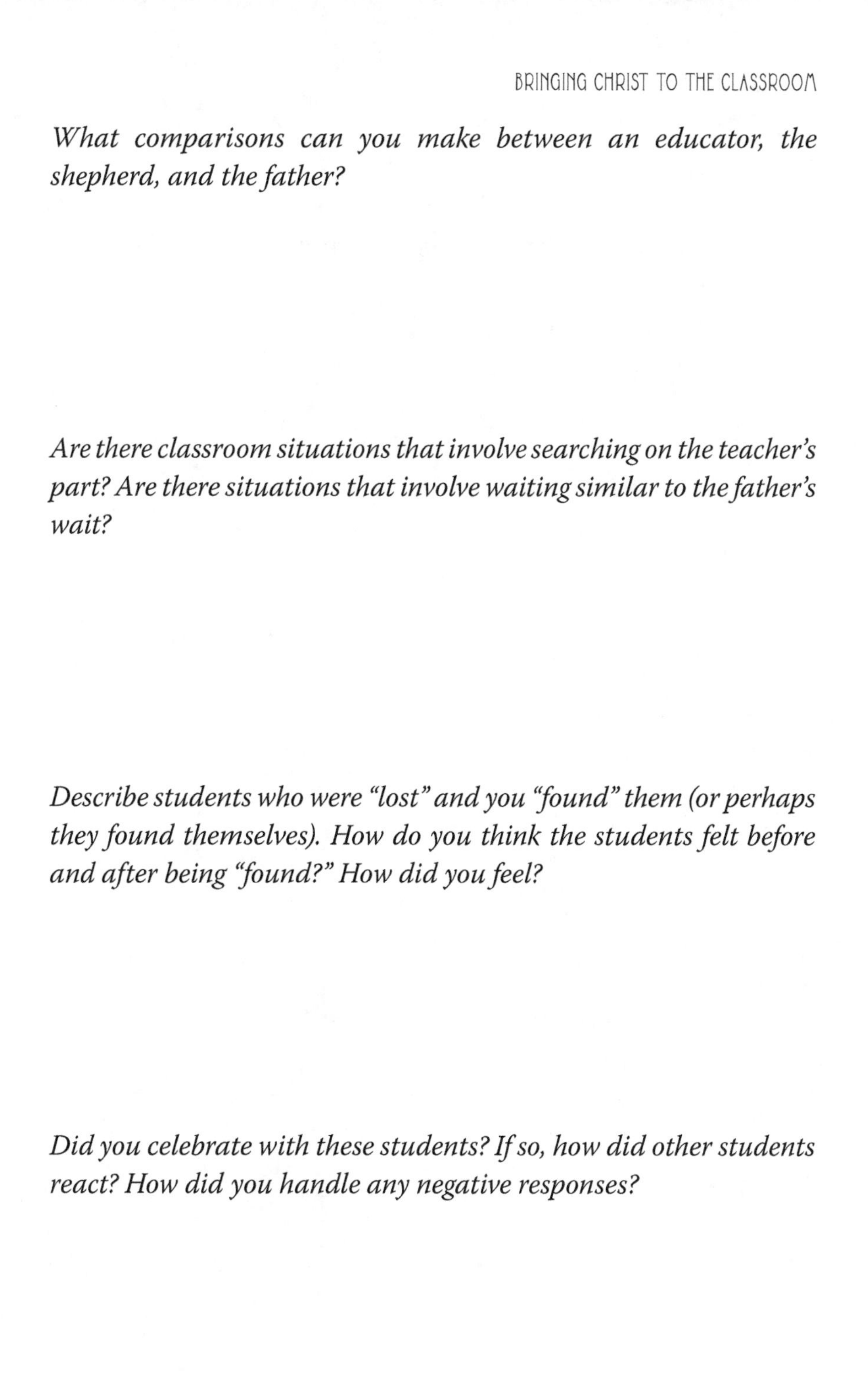

What comparisons can you make between an educator, the shepherd, and the father?

Are there classroom situations that involve searching on the teacher's part? Are there situations that involve waiting similar to the father's wait?

Describe students who were "lost" and you "found" them (or perhaps they found themselves). How do you think the students felt before and after being "found?" How did you feel?

Did you celebrate with these students? If so, how did other students react? How did you handle any negative responses?

Integrate

What insights about the searching shepherd and the father apply to your classroom?

THE SHEPHERD

"Savior like a Shepherd Lead Us"
"My Sheep Know My Voice"
"God Leads Us Along"

The restaurant was fancier than I was expecting with white linen tablecloths, real silver utensils, and multiple waiters in tuxedos hovering over every diner. My parents and I were at a Chinese restaurant in a Puerto Rican hotel where the wait staff was exceptionally attentive. Every time we drank a sip of water, someone refilled our glasses. When we put down our forks, someone took away our plates. They seemed to know what we needed before we did!

It reminds me of the experience a former student had as a nanny for a wealthy family in Europe. She noticed that the servants who lived in the basement were always present upstairs when needed by their employers, no matter the time of day or night, even if nobody signaled. When she inquired of the servants how they knew they were needed, the reply was they listened to the family members' footsteps on the wooden floors above them. They had learned to discern who was walking, where they were headed, and predict what they might need. The servants had studied their employers and knew their habits and preferences well enough to anticipate their needs and fulfill them at just the right time.[1]

Investigate

Psalm 23 portrays a similar relationship by describing the shepherd who knows the sheep well enough to anticipate their needs and fulfill them at just the right time. The shepherd knows when the sheep will be hungry or thirsty and ensures those needs are met. The shepherd leads the sheep toward green pastures and away from dangerous terrain. The shepherd knows the characteristics of each sheep. The shepherd keeps track of the sheep and seeks any who wander off.

The shepherd's main tool in caring for sheep is a staff. Author Phillip Keller makes enlightening comments about the shepherd's compassionate use of the staff. The staff has several purposes according to Keller:

1. Bringing sheep together
2. Drawing a sheep close to the shepherd for examination
3. Guiding sheep on the path
4. Holding a sheep close to the shepherd
5. Freeing sheep from entanglement[2]

How do the purposes of the shepherd's staff manifest themselves in the classroom? How does the staff contribute to a sense of belonging?

<u>Hierarchy of Needs</u>. Interesting connections can be made between the shepherd and sheep metaphor of **Psalm 23** and Abraham H. Maslow's Hierarchy of Needs. Maslow indicates that humans have

five needs which must be met for us to function in life, and until these needs are met, our motivation is to fulfill these deficiencies. These needs include survival, safety, belonging, self-esteem, and self-actualization.[3]

Read **Psalm 23.** Create a chart using the words in bold as column headings. Record your responses to these questions:

- *How are the* ***needs of the sheep*** *related to the* ***needs of students?***
- ***Maslow's Hierarchy of Needs*** *are met by the shepherd in Psalm 23?*
- *How do the* ***shepherd's provisions*** *correspond to* ***teacher's provisions*** *in the classroom?*

For example, a "prepared table" with food compatible to the sheep's dietary needs might correlate to a prepared lesson specifically designed to respectfully engage each student at their ability level. Several of Maslow's needs that would be involved in the "prepared table" classroom include:

- Safety: a classroom where risks are encouraged and mistakes are treated as learning opportunities
- Belonging: encouraged through small-group activities and respect for others
- Self-esteem: enhanced by successes and expressed appreciation for meaningful contributions

Complete your chart by analyzing several of these characteristics from Psalm 23:

- *green pastures*
- *quiet waters*

- *refreshment*
- *guides along right paths*
- *present in the darkest valley*
- *fear no evil*
- *the rod & staff*
- *a prepared table*
- *anointing*
- *overflowing cup*
- *goodness and love*

Illuminate

Use information from your chart to describe the relationship between the needs of your students and the provisions you discovered in ***Psalm 23****.*

What is the difference between student "wants" and "needs" in the classroom?

Integrate

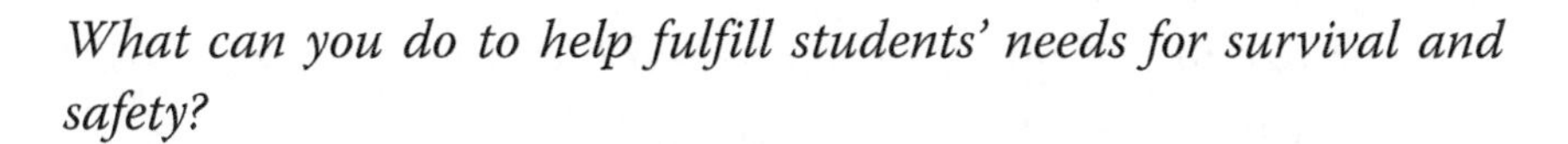

What can you do to help fulfill students' needs for survival and safety?

How can you instill a sense of belonging in each student?

How can you help students develop a healthy self-esteem?

How can you promote self-actualization within students?

How can you incorporate your discoveries into your classroom environment and your relationships with students? What potential challenges can you anticipate and what plans will you implement to minimize them? How can you help fulfill student needs at just the right time?

WAYS OF LEARNING

"I Sing the Mighty Power of God"

An underlying concept of instruction is tailoring or differentiating lessons to meet the learning needs of each student. In differentiating instruction, lessons are designed to respectfully and appropriately challenge each student. Differentiated instruction allows students to be successful by meeting their academic needs.

Another method of meeting academic needs is by implementing strategies based on preferred ways of learning, or learning styles, which are typically thought to encompass visual, auditory, kinesthetic, and tactile learning preferences. The essence of this approach is that each student prefers to learn in a unique manner. Therefore, the emphasis is on helping students understand, learn, and retain the information by incorporating into each lesson as many of these preferred ways of learning as are relevant to the topic. While some discount this approach to instruction, the book of Proverbs offers ideas worth considering when implementing students' preferred ways of learning.

Investigate

The key to meeting student learning needs is knowing the strengths of individual students. Two versions of **Proverbs 20:5** make a recommendation for discovering strengths in students:

New International Version (NIV)[1]
"The purposes of a person's heart are deep waters, but one who has insight draws them out."

The Easy-to-Read Version (ERV)[2]
"Getting information from someone can be like getting water from a deep well. If you are smart, you will draw it out."

The point of this verse is that it takes effort to learn about someone. It is like trying to get water from a well using a rope and bucket. A long rope is required to "draw out" water at the bottom of a well. When looking into a well, what is on the surface is seen but what is down deep in the well is unseen. When looking at a student, we see the surface, not what is deep inside; their thoughts, desires, and motivations are hidden. With the right knowledge, determination, and patience, we can "draw out" the hidden purposes and strengths of students, including their learning strengths.

List at least two examples of the "long rope" educators use to draw out the deep student strengths and purposes that are hidden.

Another verse that provides insight into the "drawing out" process is **Proverbs 22:6**:

New International Version (NIV)[3]
"Start children off on the way they should go, and even when they are old they will not turn from it."

Easy-to-Read Version (ERV)[4]
"Teach children in a way that fits their needs, and even when they are old, they will not leave the right path."

Amplified Bible, Classic Edition (AMPC)[5]
"Train up a child in the way he should go [and in keeping with his individual gift or bent], and when he is old he will not depart from it."

International Standard Version (ISV)[6]
"Train a child in the way appropriate for him, and when he becomes older, he will not turn from it."

The repetitive use of "train," "teach," or "start" in these versions indicates that this is an intentional process, not something left to chance. There is also the implication that this training begins early in the life of a child ("Start children off....") (NIV)[7].

In addition, we are to "Teach children in a way that fits their needs...." (ERV)[8]. That brings us back to the idea that we are to meet the needs of each child through our instruction. Appropriate instruction should be respectful of the child's God-given gifts. It should also incorporate the child's needs, personality, interests, and other characteristics.

The AMPC version of the Bible adds an interesting parenthetical comment to **Proverbs 22:6**; "... and in keeping with his individual gift or bent."[9] We know that God specifically created each of us with distinctive "bents" or inborn characteristics and abilities **(Ephesians 2:10)**, including ways of learning. It seems logical that if we approach instruction in "... the way appropriate for [students],...." (ISV)[10], and in keeping with their innate characteristics, they will thrive.

Record the "individual gifts and bents" in your current group of students.

The Amplified Bible (AMP)[11] provides a unique perspective of **Proverbs 22:6**: "Train up a child in the way he should go [teaching him to seek God's wisdom and will for his abilities and talents], Even when he is old he will not depart from it."

Not only are we to respectfully instruct students in keeping with their strengths and preferred ways of learning, we are to encourage them to pursue God's plan for using their abilities and talents.

Based on these two verses (**Proverbs 20:5** and **Proverbs 22:6**) *along with your thoughts about the above comments, pick out key words or phrases and use them to compose a sentence or two describing the tasks of educators as related to gaining insights into the ways students learn.*

Strengths Gone Awry. Despite our best efforts to build relationships with students and teach them in the ways they learn the best, not all student behavior is appropriate. Author Dr. Kathy Koch, founder and president of Celebrate Kids, Inc., in addressing multiple intelligences, offers advice that may be applied to the ways students learn when she indicates that students "in trouble" are often in that circumstance from misusing their strengths.

> Children are not necessarily stupid and not necessarily "bad," but rather have not learned self-control, self-respect, and/or respect to others. These are keys to children (and adults) being able to use their intelligence strengths for good and not evil, to help and not hurt.[15]

> When children understand the cause of the behavior that gets them into trouble, they are more empowered to change.... Children may also be encouraged to discover that improving their behavior simply requires them to use their intelligences in different ways or with less intensity to help and not hurt themselves and others.[16]

Illuminate

Learning Model. For over 40 years, Dr. Rita and Dr. Kenneth Dunn (no relation to the author of this Bible study) researched individual differences in how students learn, engage with, and retain material. They created a comprehensive model, the Dunn and Dunn Learning Style Model (available at www.learningstyles.net), which divides learning strengths into five categories or strands, each containing elements that significantly stimulate or inhibit how students learn. The elements operate on a continuum ranging from high (meaning it is a strength) to low, or from more to less. For example, some students need more structure to learn efficiently and effectively while others need less.

The elements contain, among other things, what are commonly referred to as "learning styles"—auditory, visual, tactual, and kinesthetic. The elements also encompass areas such as the learning environment, emotional factors, relationship factors, and cognitive characteristics.

The model's implementation strategy is that students should be *taught first* through their preferred ways of learning, enabling them to efficiently and effectively learn, engage with, and retain material. The next encounter with the material is through their secondary strengths. Students then produce instructional tools to reinforce their comprehension and use these tools to teach the material to their peers. This process significantly improves student learning and retention.[12]

One of the theoretical cornerstones of the Dunn and Dunn Learning Style Model is that "... given responsive environments, resources, and approaches, students attain statistically higher achievement test scores."[13] Research on implementation of the Dunn and Dunn Model at the college level supports this by revealing higher achievement and performance levels, better attitudes, less anxiety and anger, more creativity, improved quality of work, and greater retention of information.[14]

Integrate

How are your students' "gifts and bents" displayed in the instructional setting?

Describe instances when you think students' learning strengths were used in inappropriate ways. Do you think their behavior was due to misusing their strengths? In the future, how might you channel these types of inappropriate behaviors into meaningful ones?

Analyze several lessons you recently taught in light of the Dunn and Dunn Learning Style Model (found at www.learningstyles.net). *Match the components of the lessons to elements from the Dunn and Dunn model. Were several elements built into the lessons? For example, did students have options in terms of the learning environment, task structure, interaction with others, etc.? How did students respond to the lessons? How easy or difficult was it for students to understand, learn, and retain the information?*

In what ways can you intentionally create learning experiences that are respectful of your students' innate, God-given ways of learning?

WHAT WOULD JESUS DO? WWJD?

"Will Jesus Find Us Watching?"

God gave the children of Israel commands to keep them healthy, protect them from diseases, and help them lead holy lives. During the time of Jesus, the religious leaders did their best to enforce strict observance of Old Testament commands as well as customs developed through the years. The New Testament illustrates Jesus ignoring some of these customs and expectations by reaching out to help, heal, and defend those who were considered outcasts, unclean, or undesirable despite the controversy it caused.

Tax Collectors. Persons who collected Roman taxes and fixed higher tax rates than required became wealthy by keeping the profits. Therefore, tax collectors were considered greedy traitors and hated by Jews.[1] In addition, because tax collectors associated with Gentiles, they were deemed unclean.[2] Yet Jesus asked a tax collector to follow him **(Luke 5:27-32)**. In fact, Jesus was called "a friend of tax collectors and sinners" **(Matthew 11:19b)**.

Untouchables. Another group considered outcasts that Jesus interacted with were those with skin diseases, molds, and bodily discharges **(Leviticus 11-15)**. Occurrences of these situations caused the person to be "unclean" meaning he or she had to be isolated from others until declared "clean" by the priest. One could become unclean simply by touching someone with skin diseases, molds, or bodily discharges **(Leviticus 15:7)**, so the unclean were avoided. Yet Jesus touched them and healed them.

Women and Children. Other examples of Jesus' compassion for everyone included women and children. "Since Israel was a male dominated society, women's rights were sometimes overlooked."[3] "... Jewish men avoided speaking with women in public—even their own wives."[4] Yet Jesus interacted with them. Children also had a low status and were not valued. Yet Jesus used children as examples of the Kingdom.

From considering these situations, it should be clear that Jesus went against the norm of the day!

Investigate

What Would Jesus Do? Rev. Charles Sheldon's book, *In His Steps,* conveys the proposal made by a pastor who challenged his congregation to ask, "What would Jesus do?" before acting on anything and then proceed with what Jesus would do in that situation. Their challenge was to ask this question continually over an entire year.[5] Our challenge today is to determine what Jesus did in order to answer the "What would Jesus do?" question as it applies to educators.

Explore how Jesus responded to the least, the last, the lost, and the lonely by reading the following passages which demonstrate Jesus going against cultural norms and reaching out to meet the needs of those not valued. *What generalizations can you make regarding the characteristics of the people involved? How did Jesus approach these people? What commands, customs, or cultural boundaries did Jesus ignore?*

Jesus Reaches Out to Tax Collectors

1. Matthew–**Matthew 9:9-13** and **Luke 5:27-32**
2. Zacchaeus–**Luke 19:1-10**

Jesus Reaches Out to the Sick and Impaired

1. Blind–**Matthew 9:27-31, 20:29-34; Mark 8:22-26, 10:46-52;** and **John 9:1-12**
2. Peter's Mother-in-Law–**Mark 1:29-34**
3. Paralytic Man–**Mark 2:1-12**
4. Shriveled Hand–**Mark 3:1-5**
5. Deaf and Mute–**Mark 7:31-37**
6. Leprosy–**Luke 5:12-14**
7. Bleeding Woman–**Luke 8:43-48**
8. Invalid at the Pool–**John 5:5-14**

Jesus Reaches Out to the Demon Possessed

1. **Matthew 9:32-33**
2. **Mark 9:17-27**
3. **Luke 8:26-39**

Jesus Reaches Out to the Hungry

1. **Matthew 14:13-21**
2. **Matthew 15:32-39**

Jesus Reaches Out to the Marginalized

1. Children–**Matthew 18:5-14** and **Mark 10:13-16**
2. Poor Widow–**Mark 12:41-44**
3. Widow with a Dead Son–**Luke 7:11-15**
4. Sinful Woman–**Luke 7:36-50**
5. Adulteress–**John 8:2-11**

Jesus Reaches Out to Leaders

1. Jarius, Synagogue Leader–**Mark 5:21-24** and **35-43**
2. Rich Young Ruler–**Mark 10:17-22**
3. Nicodemus, Pharisee–**John 3:1**-15
4. Royal Official–**John 4:46-53**

Jesus Reaches Out to People from Other Cultures

1. Syrophoenician Woman–**Mark 7:25-30**
2. Roman Centurian–**Luke 7:1-10**
3. Samaritan Leper–**Luke 17:11-19**
4. Samaritan Woman–**John 4:4-26**

How did the people respond to Jesus? Were they surprised? What do you think was going on in their minds? What do you think produced their turning point? What, if anything, did they give up? What change in their lives occurred because of being with Jesus?

How did the disciples, religious leaders, or bystanders react to Jesus' interactions with those considered outcasts? How did Jesus respond to their comments?

Illuminate

What is the significance of Jesus' responses? What do his responses reveal about his heart?

List characteristics of your students (past or present) who would be described as least, last, lost, or lonely. Compare and contrast these characteristics with those previously listed from the Bible examples. Perhaps a Venn diagram would be helpful in organizing the characteristics.

Integrate

What did you learn about Jesus' interactions with the least, the last, the lost, and the lonely that can be applied to your classroom?

Today, what would Jesus do (WWJD)? How are you demonstrating his heart by being his hands and feet to your students? What new ways have you thought about due to your study of what Jesus did?

AFTERWORD

"Take My Life and Let It Be"

I do believe that God called you as an educator at this specific time in history, "... for such a time as this...." **(Esther 4:15)**. You will make a difference in the lives of multiple students and colleagues. God provided you with the talents, abilities, and experiences needed to serve in this capacity.

My prayer is that this study encourages you to read and examine the Bible in a different manner. Teaching is a ministry and ministry takes preparation. Use Scripture, along with the Holy Spirit's guidance, to inspire you, give you fresh ideas, and help you resolve seemingly unsolvable challenges. I pray this study will prepare you to be "... thoroughly equipped for every good work" **(2 Timothy 3:16-17)**.

I like to think of all the educators in heaven, our great cloud of witnesses, surrounding us, cheering us on, and reminding us to "... throw off everything that hinders and the sin that so easily entangles, and ... run with perseverance the race marked out for us. Let us fix our eyes on Jesus...." **(Hebrews 12:1-2a)**.

> Therefore, be clear minded and self-controlled so that you can pray. Above all, love each other deeply, because love covers a multitude of sins. Offer hospitality to one another without grumbling.

> Each one should use whatever gift he has received to serve others, faithfully administering God's grace in its various forms. If anyone serves, he should do it with the strength God provides, so that in all things God may be praised through Jesus Christ. To him be the glory and the power for ever and ever. Amen **(I Peter 4:7-11)**.

Consider that we are not guaranteed success as educators. We are, however, asked to be good stewards and dedicated followers of Christ **(I Peter 4:10-11; Hebrews 10:22-25)**. At the end of our lives, our ultimate goal is to humbly repeat what Jesus said, "I have brought you glory on earth by completing the work you gave me to do" **(John 17:4)** and then hear God say, "Well done, good and faithful servant!" **(Matthew 25:23)**. I encourage you to persevere in your service to God and your service to your students. May they recognize that you have been with Jesus.

APPENDICES

In teaching classes and working with student teachers, I developed several instruments to supplement specific topics. Three of these instruments are included as bonuses for you. Feel free to use them and pass them along as appropriate.

1. **God's Filtering System** enabled student teachers to visualize and contemplate how God uses aspects of their past to mold their present and future as well as their overall perspective.

2. The list of **Mini-Devotionals for Educators** was designed as a tool for student teachers to connect with Scripture and God each day despite their hectic schedule. The list provides weekly topical sections of 6-8 verses or short passages to ponder, one per day. They could pick and choose to study the topics most relevant to them.

3. The **Spiritual and Moral Development Chart** originated out of a need to supplement the textbook in a developmental psychology class. At the time, I was frustrated that I had not found anything to address spiritual development. I convinced Dr. Patricia Clinger, professor and chair of our Education Division at what was then Bartlesville Wesleyan College, to collaborate with me in creating this chart outlining spiritual and moral developmental milestones of

children and youth. Years later, Dawn Marie Colaw, pastor's wife and counselor at First Wesleyan Church in Bartlesville, Oklahoma, agreed to add her "Healthy God Concepts" to expand and enhance the content of this chart.

GOD'S FILTERING SYSTEM

A Toolbox of Reflections for Christian Educators

Educators know that reflection is at the heart of meeting student needs and improving instruction. To assist student teachers in reflecting on their experiences, I would bring a small wooden toolbox with toy versions of tools to help them visualize and contemplate their perspective as well as aspects of their past, present, and future. We used several metaphors in this exercise, beginning with a filter.

Filter–*establishes your perspective*

A coffee filter strains and separates the "good" from the "bad" by blocking the undesired and allowing what is pure to flow through. If you allow it, God will brew something wonderful from all of your life experiences ***(past, present, and future)*** by filtering out the "gunk" and transforming you into his image **(2 Corinthians 3:18)**. He will turn your disappointments and disasters into blessings **(Genesis 50:20)** and grant you a new attitude **(Ephesians 4:23)**. He will keep you from becoming bitter and make you better.

For Your Reflection–Your Perspective Filter

Have you thrown away the negative filter in your brain containing the undesirable, freeing yourself of life's "gunk" so you can embrace God's perspective **(Romans 12:2)**?

What "pureness" is flowing through your life to others?

Mirror–*exemplifies your past*

Mirrors are highly reflective, accurately reproducing a clear image of what is placed in front of them. Your personal mirror reflects your identity, centered on your past experiences.

For Your Reflection–The Image of Your Past Life

What do you see in your past?

Does that reflection help or hinder your future?

Are you looking at your past using God's mirror to define your present identity?

Are you currently reflecting God's image?

"But we all, who with unveiled faces, beholding as in a mirror the glory of the Lord, are being transformed into his image with ever-increasing glory, which comes from the Lord..." **(2 Corinthians 3:18)**.

Toolbox–*embodies your present*

The contents of your tool box personify what you have been equipped with via your education and experiences. These tools in your toolbox represent the **knowledge, skills, and dispositions** you have acquired that enable you to be an effective Christian educator. Are you using your God-given gifts and abilities **(Exodus 35:31)** to praise and glorify his name **(Colossians 3:17)**?

Light Bulb–The **skill** of **reflection** is required for insights–those *light-bulb moments* of wisdom. Be brilliant!

Adjustable Wrench–The wrench represents **instructional strategies** that aid you in *adjusting* to meet each student's needs. *Wrench,* when used as a noun, is a **disposition**–a surge of compassion for your students.

Needle Nose Pliers–Pliers exemplify **researched-based theories** which allow you to *pinpoint and grip* the **knowledge** relevant to the situation.

Drill–A repeating drill equates to **classroom management** which involves *repeating* many routines and procedures *(drills)* to ensure efficient use of time, space, supplies, and equipment. Managing a classroom well comes from **skills** and experience.

Chisel–**Classroom management** also entails chiseling or *smoothing the rough edges* of students as well as yourself. Many students need to be viewed as "diamonds in the rough."

Screw Driver–Several general **classroom management** tasks can be likened to the screw driver whose duties include strengthening *(tightening)*, securing *(fastening)*, and compelling *(putting on the pressure)* in a variety of situations.

For your Reflection about your Past and Present:

> The facts about what happen do not define us; *how we react and how we think about the event* make us who and what we are.
>
> How has God used your *past* and *present* for his glory?

Window–*epitomizes your future potential*

The window of your life opens to limitless future opportunities. It takes faith and courage to give your future to God and follow where he guides.

For your Reflection about your Future View:

> Is your window wide open to God's leading?
>
> Be encouraged by the fact that you are his "handiwork, created in Christ Jesus to do good works, which God prepared in advance for [you] to do" **(Ephesians 2:10)**.
>
> Are you serving God whole-heartedly **(Ephesians 6:7; Colossians 3:23)**?

MINI-DEVOTIONALS FOR EDUCATORS

1 Topic Per Week
1-2 Focus Passages Per Day

Allow God to Mold You Through Adversity

- Jeremiah 18:1-10–Be moldable in adversity
- Romans 6:18-30–Present sufferings; future glory
- Philippians 4:11-13–The secret of contentment
- 1 Thessalonians 5:18–Thanks in all circumstances
- 2 Thessalonians 1:4b-5–Counted worthy
- 2 Timothy 2:25–Gentle instruction
- Hebrews 12:7-11–Discipline's harvest
- James 1:2-4–Testing of your faith

Attitude of Gratitude

- Psalm 35:18–Where to be thankful
- Psalm 100:4–Enter with thanksgiving
- 1 Chronicles 16:34–Why we are thankful
- Luke 17:11-19–Importance of saying "thank you"
- Colossians 3:15-16–Gratitude in your heart
- 1 Thessalonians 5:16-18–Thankful in all

Bad Things Happen to Good People

- 2 Timothy 3:12-14–Christians will be persecuted
- Matthew 5:44-45–It rains on the righteous and the unrighteous

Be Generous

- Proverbs 22:9–Share with the poor
- Malachi 3:10-11–Heaven's floodgates of blessing open
- John 3:16–God gave
- 2 Corinthians 8:7–Excel in the grace of giving
- 2 Corinthians 9:6-11–Sow generously, cheerfully
- 1 Timothy 6:18–Be generous, willing to share

Be God' Light

- Psalm 27:1–The Lord is my light and salvation
- Matthew 5:14-16–Jesus said you are to be the light of the world
- John 8:12–Jesus is the Light of the world
- Ephesians 5:6-20–Live as a child of Light
- Philippians 2:15-16–Shine like a star
- 1 John 1:5-10–Walking in the Light
- Revelation 22:5–God will be our Light

Be Godly

- Deuteronomy 10:12-13–Walk in His ways
- Micah 6:8–What God requires
- Ephesians 4:1-6–Live a life worthy of your calling
- Colossians 1:10–Live a life worthy of the Lord
- 1 Timothy 2:1-4–Seek the Lord's peace
- 1 Peter 1:13-16–Be holy
- 1 Peter 2:11-12–Live so that God will be glorified

Be Willing to be God's Hands and Feet

- Joshua 14:6-12–Follow God wholeheartedly
- 1 Samuel 15:22; 16:7–God desires obedience and looks at the heart

- Ecclesiastes 3:1-14–Everything made beautiful; God sets eternity in students' hearts
- Isaiah 52:7–Bring good news; proclaim peace, salvation
- Matthew 6:1-4–Give in secret
- Matthew 13:24-32–Sow seeds of truth, despite the weeds—one may be a mustard seed!
- Luke 10:30-37–Take care of those who cannot care for themselves

The Christian's Character

- Galatians 5:22-26–Fruit of the Spirit
- Philippians 4:8-9–Think about such things
- Colossians 3:12-17–Clothe yourself with these virtues
- Colossians 4:2-4–Devote yourselves to prayer
- 1 Thessalonians 4:1-12; 5:12-15–Lead a quiet, peaceful life
- 2 Peter 1:5-10–Possess these qualities in increasing measure
- 1 Timothy 2:1-3; 8–Peaceful, quiet lives

Confirm Your Calling

- Isaiah 41:9-10–Called, upheld
- Matthew 4:18-22; Mark 1:16-20; Mark 8:34-38–Be willing to follow Jesus
- Romans 12:1–Offer yourself as a living sacrifice
- Ephesians 2:10–Our work is prepared in advance
- Ephesians 4:1–Live worthy of your calling
- 1 Timothy 4:12–Be an example
- 2 Timothy 2:15; 20-21–Present yourself to God as a useful vessel

Do Not Be Afraid

- Exodus 14:13-14; II Chronicles 20:17 and 32:7-8–The Lord will fight for you

- Deuteronomy 31:6-8; Joshua 1:7-9–God goes with you so be strong and courageous
- Psalm 34:4–God will deliver you from your fears
- Psalm 34:7–Angels encamp
- Jeremiah 1:8–God rescues
- Daniel 10:11–God hears and responds when we humble ourselves
- Zephaniah 3:17–God delights in you
- Mark 4:35-40–With you through life's storms

Forgive

- Matthew 6:14-15–Forgive, so you will be forgiven
- Matthew 18:21-35–Forgive from your heart
- Mark 11:25–If you hold anything against anyone
- Luke 6:37–Forgive and you'll be forgiven
- Luke 17:3-4–How often should you forgive?
- Luke 23:34–Forgive, as Jesus forgave
- Colossians 3:13–Forgive anyone who offends you

Give it to God

- Genesis 22:1-18–God will provide what you need
- Psalm 55:22; John 14:1; I Peter 5:7–Give cares to God
- Psalm 125:1-2–Trust in the Lord
- Proverbs 3:5-6; Isaiah 55:8-9–Trust God rather than your own understanding
- Proverbs 16:9–Let God determine your steps
- Isaiah 26:3-4–Perfect peace
- Matthew 6:25-39–Do not worry

Give Your Best to The Master

- 1 Chronicles 28:9–Wholehearted devotion
- 1 Chronicles 28:20–Do the work, God is with you

- Proverbs 6:6-8–The example of the ant
- Proverbs 13:4–Be diligent
- Matthew 16:27; I Corinthians 3:5-15–Rewarded according to what you do
- Matthew 22:37-8–Love God with everything
- Matthew 25:21–Faithful servant
- 2 Corinthians 5:9-10; Ephesians 6:5-8–The goal is to please God
- Galatians 6:9–Do not weary in doing good
- Ephesians 2:10–Created to do good works
- Ephesians 6:7–Wholeheartedly serve the Lord
- Colossians 3:37–Do everything in Jesus' name
- Colossians 3:22-24–Work with all your heart
- 2 Timothy 2:15–Present yourself to God as one approved

God is our Strength

- Deuteronomy 33:27–Everlasting arms
- 2 Chronicles 16:9–God strengthens those who are fully committed to him
- Psalm 37:23–God upholds us
- Psalm 46:1-2–God is our refuge
- Isaiah 40:28-31–God gives strength to the weary
- Zechariah 4:6–By his Spirit
- Ephesians 6:10-17–God's armor is ours

God Knows You

- Psalm 139:2-3–He knows where you are, what you're thinking, and what you will say—24/7
- Psalm 139:7-10–His presence is with you wherever you go
- Psalm 139:13–He created you
- Psalm 139:15-16–He knew you from before you were born; ordained all the days of your life
- Isaiah 49:16–Your name is written on the palms of his hands

- Hebrews 4:13–He looks into your soul
- Revelation 2:17–He will give you a new name known only to you and to him

God Sends Darkness, for a Time

- Genesis 1:2–Darkness was on the face of the deep
- Exodus 10:21-24–God uses plague of darkness to work on Pharaoh's heart
- Exodus 13:21–Pillar of fire lights the darkness for the Israelites
- Exodus 24:15-18–Darkness allowed Moses to ascend the mountain and meet with God
- Isaiah 9:2–Walking in darkness
- Isaiah 45:7–God forms the light and the darkness
- Luke 23:44-45–Darkness over entire earth at Jesus' death
- 1 Peter 2:9–You are called out of darkness

God Uses the Ordinary in Extraordinary Ways

- Exodus 6:28-7:5–Moses argued about his limitations
- Judges 6:11-16–Gideon doubted and argued about his lowly position
- 1 Samuel 3–God uses a boy
- 1 Samuel 16:11-13–God chose a young sheep herder
- 1 Samuel 17:41-58–An obedient boy with a slingshot slays the giant
- Isaiah 6:8–Here am I, Send me
- Acts 26:13-19–Saul obeys the vision from heaven

Heroes of the Faith Go Through Adversity

- Genesis 37:23-28; 39:16-20; 45:1-15; 50:15-21–Joseph sees the big picture
- Ruth 1:1-16; 4:13-15–Ruth chose Naomi's God
- 1 Samuel 1:1-2:11–Hannah praises God for answering

- Job 1:21; 13:15; 19:25-27; 23:10-12–The Lord gives, the Lord takes away
- Daniel 1:3-6; 3:16-18–Israelite boys trust God
- Jonah 1:1-3:3–Jonah learns obedience the hard way
- 2 Corinthians 12:7-10–Paul's strength in weakness

Jesus' Divine Nature

- Isaiah 9:6–Wonderful, Counselor, Mighty God
- Matthew 18:20–Omni-presence
- Mark 2:7–Forgives our sins
- Mark 4:39; 5:29–Power over nature, life
- John 1:3–Through him all things were made
- Colossians 1:37–In him all things hold together
- Hebrews 1:3–Son radiates God's glory

Jesus' Emotions

- Matthew 13:54-58–Hometown took offense
- Matthew 21:12-13; John 2:13-16–Upset
- Matthew 26:37-8–Sorrowful, troubled, overwhelmed
- Luke 22:1-6–Betrayed
- Luke 22:54-61–Let down
- John 11:33-35–Cried at death of friend
- John 12:27–Troubled heart

Jesus' Human Nature

- Galatians 4:4–Born of a woman
- 1 Timothy 3:15–Incarnate
- Luke 2:40; 2:52–Grew up
- Luke 24:39–Human body–flesh and bones
- Hebrews 5:7-8–Learned obedience from suffering
- Luke 22:44–Anguished in prayer

Jesus' Ministries

- *Perfect Sacrifice*–Hebrews 7:27; Revelation 5:9–His blood purchased you for God
- *Effective Priest*–Hebrews 7:23-26–Jesus intercedes for us
- *Eternal King*–Revelation 5:12-13–Worthy is the Lamb
- *Healer*–Matthew 4:23-24; 8:16-17–healed the blind, lame, sick; took up our infirmities
- *Life-Giver*–John 11:43-44–Lazarus
- *Master Evangelist*–(a) crowds–Matthew 5:1-2; (b) individuals–John 3:3
- *Rabbi*–Mark 6:34–Compassionate teacher
- *Ruler over nature*–Mark 11:20-21 (fig tree); Mark 4:39 (wind and waves)

Jesus Promised to Come Back

- Matthew 24:36-51–Keep watch–unknown when
- Matthew 25:1-13–Keep watch–be prepared
- John 14:1-3–Jesus is preparing a place for you
- 1 Thessalonians 4:16-18–Caught up to meet the Lord
- Revelation 19:11-17–Jesus returns!
- Revelation 21:1-7–God dwelling with men
- Revelation 21:22-27–No need for a temple

Jesus Understands (Hebrews 4:15)

- Matthew 8:20–No place to lay his head
- Mark 1:13–Tempted
- Mark 15:19-20–Mocked
- John 2:15-16–Angry
- John 4:6–Weary, thirsty, hungry
- John 6:66–Followers left
- Matthew 26:14-16; 45; 48-49–Betrayed
- Matthew 26:38–Full of sorrow
- Matthew 27:46–Forsaken by God

Let Us Adore Him

- Psalm 8; Nehemiah 9:6–Praise to the Creator of nature
- Psalm 13:5-6–God's love never fails
- Psalm 47–Praise to the King
- Psalm 84–Praise God in his dwelling place
- Psalm 100–Shout for joy
- Psalm 103-104–Praise for who he is, what he does
- Psalm 139–Praise the One who thought about you before you were born

New Life

- Isaiah 62:1-3; Revelation 2:17–Called by new name
- Ezekiel 11:19-20; 18:30-32; 36:25-27–Undivided heart and new spirit
- Romans 12:2; Ephesians 4:22-24–Renew your mind
- Colossians 3:1-10–Set your heart and mind on things above
- 2 Corinthians 4:16–Inwardly renewed
- 2 Corinthians 5:17–All things are new
- 1 Peter 1:2-4–New birth into a living hope

Precious Promises (II Peter 1:4)

- Psalm 23–If you are afraid, he is with you
- Psalm 126:5-6–If you sow in tears, you will reap in joy
- Matthew 11:28–If you need rest, he will provide it
- 1 Corinthians 10:13–God will help you stand under temptation
- 2 Thessalonians 3:3–If you need strength to resist the evil one, he will provide it
- Hebrews 13:5–God will never leave or forsake you
- James 4:8–If you draw near to God, he will draw near to you

Pray Until God Moves

- Psalm 5:1-3–Pray daily
- Psalm 102:1-2–Call out to God
- Jeremiah 29:12–God listens when we pray
- Jeremiah 33:3–Call and he will answer
- Ephesians 6:18–Pray in the Spirit on all occasions
- Philippians 4:6-7–Present your requests to God
- 1 Thessalonians 5:16-17–Pray continually

Seek God

- Psalm 37:7a and 46:10; Lamentations 3:25-26–Be still before the Lord
- Psalm 42:1–Desire God
- Psalm 51:10-12–Seek a pure heart
- Isaiah 55:6-7–Seek God while he may be found
- Jeremiah 29:13–Seek with all your heart
- John 15:1-8–Remain in Jesus
- James 5:13-16–The prayer of faith

Seek Wisdom

- Proverbs 1:8-9–Let instruction be your garland
- Proverbs 1:28-33–Seek wisdom–or learn the hard way
- Proverbs 8:10-11–Wisdom is precious
- Proverbs 13:13-14–Respect the teaching of the wise
- Isaiah 55:8-9–God's wisdom transcends all
- Ephesians 1:17-18–Spirit of wisdom
- James 3:13-18–Heavenly wisdom

Serve Willingly

- Matthew 20:25-28–Serve, no matter your position
- John 13:12-17–Jesus modeled service

- 1 Corinthians 12:4-5–Different kinds of service
- Galatians 5:13–Serve in love
- Ephesians 6:7–Serve wholeheartedly
- Philippians 2:1-8–Serve with Jesus' attitude
- 1 Peter 4:10–Serve with your gifts

Sleep in Heavenly Peace

- Psalm 3:5–The Lord sustains
- Psalm 4:8–Safe and peaceful sleep
- Psalm 127:2–Sleep for God's beloved
- Proverbs 3:21-24–Sweet sleep
- Ecclesiastes 5:12–Sleep of the worker
- John 14:27; 16:33–Jesus gives peace because he overcame the world

Watch Your Words (spoken, written, or texted)

- Proverbs 12:13-14, 18-19, 22, 25–Tongue of the wise
- Proverbs 15:1-2; Proverbs 25:11; Colossians 4:6–A gentle answer, aptly spoken
- Proverbs 15:4–The healing tongue
- Proverbs 13:3; 21:23–Guard your tongue
- Ecclesiastes 5:1-3–Listen to God; let words be few
- Matthew 12:34-37–Beware of careless words
- James 3:3-12–The tongue needs taming

Working with People

- Romans 12:10–Honor others over yourself
- Romans 12:12–Be prayerfully patient
- Romans 12:14–Bless your persecutors
- Romans 12:16–Live in harmony; be humble
- Romans 12:19–Do not take revenge
- Romans 12:21–Overcome evil with good

You Can Control Your Response

- Matthew 5:43-48; 22:36-39–Love & pray for everyone
- Matthew 7:1-5–Do not judge
- Matthew 18:15-17–When you are sinned against
- Matthew 24:10-13–Do not grow cold, no matter what others do
- Romans 12:17-21; 2 Thessalonians 5:12-18; James 3:18–Live at peace with everyone
- 1 Corinthians 10:23-24–Seek the good of others
- 2 Corinthians 10:5–Take captive every thought
- Galatians 6:7-10–You reap what you sow; do not be weary in doing good

SPIRITUAL & MORAL DEVELOPMENT

Dr. Patricia Clinger, Charissa Dunn, and Dawn Marie Colaw

Ages	Spiritual & Moral Characteristics	Parenting Responsibilities	Spiritual Training	Healthy God Concepts*
0-2	• Depends on others for survival • Requires unconditional love • Learns boundaries • Learns who controls boundaries • Learns about disapproval • Shows signs of empathy toward others	• Model Christ • Show unconditional love • Show steadiness, dependability of love • Satisfy needs • Provide nourishment • Keep them from harm • Keep them from harming each other	• Lay groundwork for spiritual framework • God's wonders in nature • Secure boundaries in God's law • God's love and dependability • Literal simplicity of Bible stories	***Nurturing God:*** El-Shaddai Genesis 17:1-2 Psalm 22:9 Psalm 131:2
2-3	• Begins to show signs of guilt for misdeeds • Seeks control	• Model Christ • Model forgiveness • Show God through love and constancy • Momma and Daddy love you	• Repetition of concrete truths • Creator loves and cares for you • Use senses to convey truths • Begin training in prayer and stewardship	***Comforting God:*** Abba-Daddy Mark 14:36 Romans 8:15 Galatians 4:6
3-5	• Learns to do good to others—if it benefits self • Has imaginative beliefs • Feels guilt for misdeeds • Trusts others	• Model Christian behavior toward others (you cannot harm yourself or others) • Model dependability • Love them for who they are, not what they do • Train to respect and obey parents, teachers, and God	• Learn of God through nature • Plant the seeds for faith and godly attitudes • God is awesome, powerful, unchanging, and forgiving • You can trust God in all situations • Prayer • Scripture memorization	***Forgiving God:*** Jehovah Genesis 3:8 John 3:16

6-12	• Has a literal, simplistic, inquisitive faith • Respects rules • Seeks approval of others • Performs altruistic acts—for praise • Has a reward and punishment perspective <u>Older</u>: • Internalizes parents' moral standards • Is a hero-worshipper • 12 – 13 = Age of accountability	• Model Christian behavior toward others • Encourage daily personal devotions • Parents are given responsibility from God to instill moral values • There are rights, wrongs—based on God's Word • Train to respect and obey parents, teachers, and God • Promote Christian heroes, saints	• God expects us to be responsible for our own behavior • Principles of Christianity • Majesty, power, and holiness of God • Mercy to others • True stories of saints, Jesus, etc. • The inspired Word of God as the daily guidebook • Salvation • Prayer • Scripture memorization	***<u>Sympathizing God</u>:*** Great High Priest Hebrews 4:15-16
12-18	• Tries out different value systems • Searches for personal identity • Experiments with internal moral codes • Conforms to peer morals • Abstract reasoning about morals is possible • Responds sympathetically • Feels guilt for not responding	• Model a personal relationship with God • Transfer responsibility to child (a slow process) in the context of God's will • Afford freedom within boundaries • Offer assurances of love, support and protection • Impart a balance between trust and worthy of trust	• Salvation, Trinity, prayer, and Scripture memorization • Responsible to God for self and for others • Christian world view • Prevenient will of God • God's power and forgiveness • Christian principles and philosophy	***<u>Reliable God</u>:*** Jehovah Shammah Father of the Prodigal Luke 15:18-24 Great I AM Exodus 3:14-15

*Healthy God Concepts to teach and learn were developed by Dawn Marie Colaw.

ENDNOTES

Faith Matters

Called to Teach?

1 Miller, Dan. "Transformed by a Dream." *AARP The Magazine,* November-December 2007, p. 88. Copyright 2007 AARP. All rights reserved. Used by permission.
2 Taken from *If You Want to Walk on Water, You've Got to Get Out of the Boat* by John Ortberg. Copyright © 2001, p. 60 by John Ortberg. Use by permission of Zondervan. www.zondervan.com
3 Ibid., p. 63.
4 Ibid., p. 71.
5 Ibid., p. 61.
6 Taken from *My Utmost for His Highest®* by Oswald Chambers, © 1935 by Dodd Mead & Co., p. 65, renewed © 1963 by the Oswald Chambers Publications Assn., Ltd. Print. Used by permission of Discovery House, Grand Rapids, MI 49501. All rights reserved.
7 Van Dyk, John. *The Craft of Christian Teaching: A Classroom Journey.* Sioux Center: Dordt Press, 2000, pp. 35-36. Print. Used by permission.

Faith and Learning

1 Clinger, Patricia. Student Teaching Seminar. Bartlesville, Oklahoma. Spring 2000. Used by permission.
2 Taken from *Sacred Pathways: Discovering Your Soul's Path to God* by Gary Thomas. Copyright © 1996, p. 23 by Gary Thomas. Use by permission of Zondervan. www.zondervan.com

Light of the World

1 Hughes, Steve. Sunday School Presentation. First Wesleyan Church. Bartlesville, Oklahoma. Used by permission.

Made in His Image

1 Koch, Kathy. *What We See is What They Get.* Mill Valley: Continuum, Golden Gate Seminary, 1997, p. 12. Print.

Prayer

1 Hostetler, Bob. "31 Ways to Pray for Your Kids." App and prayer card may be purchased at: http://www.bobhostetler.com/31-ways-to-pray-app

Salt

1 Clarke, Adam, and Ralph Earle. *Adam Clarke's Commentary on the Bible.* Grand Rapids: Baker Book House, 1967, p. 154. Print.
2 Eskew, Garnett Laidlaw. *Salt, the Fifth Element: The Story of a Basic American Industry.* Chicago: J. G. Ferguson and Associates, 1948, pp. 203-223. Print.
3 Taken from *The Parables,* © 1991, p. 90, by Gary Inrig. Used by permission of Discovery House Publishers, Grand Rapids MI 49501. All rights reserved.

Instructional Strategies from The Master

Assessment

1 Covey, Stephen R. *The 7 Habits of Highly Effective People.* New York: Simon & Schuster, 1989, 2004, 102. Print.

Conversations with Jesus

1 Zuck, Roy B. *Teaching as Jesus Taught.* Grand Rapids: Baker Books, 1995, p. 173. Print. Used by permission of Wipf and Stock Publishers. www.wipfandstock.com

Metaphors

1 Zuck, Roy B. *Teaching as Jesus Taught.* Grand Rapids: Baker Books, 1995, p. 186. Print. Used by permission of Wipf and Stock Publishers. www.wipfandstock.com

Questions Jesus Asked

1 Bloom, Benjamin S., ed., *Taxonomy of Educational Objectives.* New York: David McKay Company, Inc., 1956, p. 18. Print.
2 Zuck, Roy B. *Teaching as Jesus Taught.* Grand Rapids: Baker Books, 1995, pp. 258-276. Print. Used by permission of Wipf and Stock Publishers. www.wipfandstock.com

Responses to Questions

1 Gilliland, Hap. *Teaching the Native American.* 3rd ed. Dubuque: Kendall/Hunt Publishing Company, 1995, pp. 33-49. Print.
2 Mehrabian, Albert. *Silent Messages.* Belmont: Wadsworth Publishing Company, Inc., 1971, p. 43. Print.
3 Zuck, Roy B. *Teaching as Jesus Taught.* Grand Rapids: Baker Books, 1995, pp. 258-276. Print. Used by permission of Wipf and Stock Publishers. www.wipfandstock.com

The Woman at the Well

1 Koch, Kathy. *Finding Authentic Hope and Wholeness: 5 Questions That Will Change Your Life.* Chicago: Moody Publishers, 2005, p. 14. Print. Used by permission.
2 Ibid., p. 14.

Relationships and Student Essentials

Belonging

1 Williams, Margery. *The Velveteen Rabbit.* New York: Delacorte Press, 1922, p. 8. Print.
2 Munsch, Robert. *Love You Forever.* Willowdale: Firefly Books Ltd. 1986. Print.

3 de Saint Exupery, Antonine. *The Little Prince.* San Diego: Harcourt Brace Jovanovich, Publishers, 1943, p.80. Print.
4 Maslow, Abraham H. *Motivation and Personality.* New York: Harper & Row, 1970, p. 35-47. Print.
5 Erikson, Erik H. *The Life Cycle Completed: A Review.* New York: W.W. Norton and Company, 1982, p. 70. Print.
6 Some content taken from *See Yourself as God Sees You* by Josh McDowell. Copyright © 1999, pp. 100-106. Used by permission of Tyndale House Publishers, Inc. All rights reserved.
7 Koch, Kathy. *Finding Authentic Hope and Wholeness: 5 Questions That Will Change Your Life.* Chicago: Moody Publishers, 2005, p. 14. Print. Used by permission.
8 Clark, Chap and Dee Clark. *Disconnected: Parenting Teens in a MySpace World.* Grand Rapids: Baker Books, 2007, p. 54. Print.

Community

1 Chapman, Gary. *The 5 Love Languages: The Secret to Love That Lasts.* Chicago: Northfield Publishing, 2010. Print.

Compassionate Shepherd

1 *Dictionary.com.* Dictionary.com, n.d. Web. 27 July 2015.
2 Jennings, Patricia A. *Mindfulness for Teachers: Simple Skills for Peace and Productivity in the Classroom.* New York: W. W. Norton & Company. 2015, p. 127. Print. Used by permission.
3 Ibid., p. 76.

Emotions

1 Goleman, Daniel. *Emotional Intelligence.* New York: Bantam Books, 1994, p. 43. Print.
2 Jensen, Eric. *Teaching with Poverty in Mind.* Alexandria: ASCD. 2009, p. 18. Print.
3 Bocchino, Rob. *Emotional Literacy: To Be a Different Kind of Smart.* Thousand Oaks: Corwin Press, Inc., 1999, p. 11. Print.
4 Gottman, John. *Raising an Emotionally Intelligent Child: The Heart of Parenting.* New York: Simon & Schuster Paperbacks, 1997, p. 21. Print.

Encouragement

1 Rath, Tom and Donald O. Clifton. *How Full is Your Bucket?* New York: Gallup Press, 2009, p. 5. Print.

Feed My Lambs

1 Clarke, Adam, and Ralph Earle. *Adam Clarke's Commentary on the Bible.* Grand Rapids: Baker Book House, 1967, p. 955. Print.
2 Taken from *A Shepherd Looks at Psalm 23* by Phillip W. Keller Copyright © 1970, p. 17 by Phillip W. Keller. Use by permission of Zondervan. www.zondervan.com
3 Ibid., p. 31.
4 Ibid., p. 35.

Identity

1 Erikson, Erik H. *The Life Cycle Completed: A Review.* New York: W.W. Norton and Company, 1982, p. 75. Print.
2 Clark, Chap and Dee Clark. *Disconnected: Parenting Teens in a MySpace World.* Grand Rapids: Baker Books, 2007, p. 56. Print.
3 Ibid., pp. 55-56.
4 Luft, Joseph. Of Human Interaction. Palo Alto: National Press Books, 1969, p. 13. Print. Used by permission.
5 Ibid., p. 22.
6 Ibid., p. 45.
7 Cooley, Charles Horton. *Human Nature and the Social Order.* New York: Schocken Books, 1964, p. 184. Print.
8 Some content taken from *PARENTING WITH LOVE AND LOGIC,* by Foster Cline and Jim Fay. Copyright © 1990, 2006, p. 35. Used by permission of NavPress. All rights reserved. Represented by Tyndale House Publishers, Inc.
9 Some content taken from *See Yourself as God Sees You* by Josh McDowell. Copyright © 1999, pp. 166-167. Used by permission of Tyndale House Publishers, Inc. All rights reserved.
10 Koch, Kathy. *What We See is What They Get.* Mill Valley: Continuum, Golden Gate Seminary, 1997, p. 12. Print.

Safe Haven

1. Linn, Dennis, Sheila Fabricant Linn and Matthew Linn. *Sleeping with Bread: Holding What Gives You Life.* Mahwah: Paulist Press, 1994, p. 1. Print. Used by permission.
2. Purkey, William Watson and John M. Novak. *Inviting School Success: A Self-Concept Approach to Teaching, Learning, and Democratic Practice.* Belmont: Wadsworth Publishing Company, 1996. Print.
3. Stronks, Julie K. and Gloria Goris Stronks. *Christian Teachers in Public Schools.* Grand Rapids: Baker Books, 1999, p. 53-54. Print.
4. Costello, Bob, Joshua Wachtel and Ted Wachtel. *The Restorative Practices Handbook for Teachers, Disciplinarians and Administrators.* Bethlehem: International Institute for Restorative Practices Graduate School, www.iirp.edu, 2009, p. 7. Print. Used by permission.
5. Ibid., p. 14.
6. Ibid., p. 13.
7. Ibid., p. 51.

The Shepherd

1. Maydew, Tera. Student Testimonial. School of Education Commissioning. Oklahoma Wesleyan University. Bartlesville, Oklahoma, May 13, 2011. Used by permission.
2. Taken from *A Shepherd Looks at Psalm 23* by Phillip W. Keller Copyright © 1970, pp. 100-103 by Phillip W. Keller. Use by permission of Zondervan. www.zondervan.com
3. Maslow, Abraham H. *Motivation and Personality.* New York: Harper & Row, 1970 pp. 35-47. Print.

Ways of Learning

1. Scripture is taken from the Holy Bible, NEW INTERNATIONAL VERSION®, NIV® Copyright © 1973, 1978, 1984, 2011 by Biblica, Inc.® Used by permission. All rights reserved worldwide.
2. Scripture quotations marked (ERV) are taken from the HOLY BIBLE: EASY-TO-READ VERSION © 2014 by Bible League International. Used by permission.
3. NIV op. cit
4. ERV op. cit.

5 Scripture quotations taken from the Amplified® Bible (AMPC), Copyright © 1954, 1958, 1962, 1964, 1965, 1987 by The Lockman Foundation. Used by permission. www.Lockman.org
6 Scripture quotations marked (ISV) are taken from the Holy Bible: International Standard Version® Release 2.0. Copyright © 1996-2017 by the ISV Foundation. Used by permission of Davidson Press, LLC. ALL RIGHTS RESERVED INTERNATIONALLY.
7 NIV op. cit.
8 ERV op. cit.
9 AMPC op. cit.
10 ISV op. cit.
11 AMPC op. cit.
12 Favre, Lois and Karen Russo. *Bound for Success: Individualizing Learning through Learning-Style Strengths and Strategies. Learning Styles: Online Learning Style Assessments & Community.* N.p. Copyright 2007-11. Web. 23 May 2016. www.learningstyles.net. Used by permission.
13 Ibid.
14 Russo, Karen. "Using Non-Traditional Instructional Materials to Inspire and Educate Preservice Teachers." Learning Styles Institute Symposium. Northeastern State University, Tahlequah. July 2011. Address. Used by permission.
15 Koch, Kathy. *How Am I Smart? A Parent's Gide to Multiple Intelligences.* Chicago: Moody Publishers, 2007, p. 24. Print. Used by permission.
16 Ibid., p. 23.

What Would Jesus Do?

1 Packer, J. I., Merrill C. Tenney, and William White. *The Bible Almanac.* Nashville: T. Nelson, 1980, pp. 529-530. Print.
2 Taken from *The Parables,* © 1991, p. 11, by Gary Inrig. Used by permission of Discovery House Publishers, Grand Rapids, MI 49501. All rights reserved.
3 Packer, op. cit., 421.
4 Borchert, Gerald L. *The New American Commentary: An Exegetical and Theological Exposition of Holy Scripture.* Nashville: Broadman & Holman Publishers, 1996, p. 202. Print.
5 Sheldon, Charles M. *In His Steps.* Westwood: Fleming H. Revel Company, 1963, p. 16. Print.

CPSIA information can be obtained
at www.ICGtesting.com
Printed in the USA
LVHW080222060519
616746LV00019B/296/P

9 781532 054785